The
Case Against
Having Children

The
Case Against
Having Children

by
Anna and
Arnold Silverman

DAVID McKAY COMPANY, INC.

New York

THE CASE AGAINST HAVING CHILDREN

LIBRARY OF CONGRESS CATALOG CARD NUMBER: 74-159821
MANUFACTURED IN THE UNITED STATES OF AMERICA

TO OUR PARENTS

ACKNOWLEDGMENTS

We would like to extend our thanks and gratitude to Professor Ethel Alpenfels, Dr. Richard Radkin, Dr. Henry Haberfeld, Dr. Rebecca Liswood, Dr. O. J. Miller, Mr. Ira Neiger, Miss Judy Senderowitz, Dr. Richard Hausknecth, Mrs. Janice LaRoche, Dr. Dan Dodson, Dr. Robert Gould, Dr. Margaret Mead, Dr. Anthony Summo, and the authors of the books and articles quoted herein.

And our special thanks to Dr. Thomas Gilbart.

Contents

The
Case Against
Having Children

I

The Myth of
the Maternal Instinct

Mankind has existed on earth for some two million years and for most of that time the *only* thing that differentiated men from women was the childbearing and childfeeding capability of the female. Professor Ethel Alpenfels of the New York University Department of Educational Anthropology explains that many of the earliest male fossils discovered were not men at all but women mistaken for men because of their large bone structure. "It was difficult to tell from those early fossils which were males or females," Professor Alpenfels said, "because men and women were the same size. This could indicate that women worked hard, hunted with men, and traveled and suffered death on the trail just as men did."

This picture of women at the beginning of the human epoch as aggressive hunters, powerful nomads, and co-partners with men in the struggle for survival in a hostile environment is a 180-degree turn from the more recent

1

view of women as docile, weak, submissive creatures who must rely on their men for protection and the essentials of life. What happened to bring about this metamorphosis? In a word, civilization with its religious, political, social, and legal institutions, each of which added a link to the chain of repressive and restrictive conditions that now relegate women to a secondary position in the pattern of human relations. The very first link forged in that chain was the institutionalization of motherhood, the notion that bearing and raising children was, to the exclusion of most other functions, a woman's major "purpose." Somewhat later in history, the anchor for the chain was fashioned. The Myth of the Maternal Instinct, the idea that a woman *must* have children or forfeit her true role in life.

In the beginning man roamed over earth defending himself against attackers, searching for food, and leading a day-to-day existence in a savage world. During these wanderings he had little reason to specialize in any particular job. Everyone, women included, had to be a jack-of-all-trades in order for the band to survive. It would have been impractical and indeed unthinkable for strong young women to stay behind to play with babies when attackers threatened or when the hunt was on. Women had their babies on the trail and left them to be cared for by the older clan members. In those days only the bands that could muster the most hunters and warriors survived and females, making up half of the clan, had to do their part. Because of the great demands made on them, a form of natural selection took place. Only those strong enough to survive grew to adulthood and reproduced themselves which probably accounts for the initial equality in size between males and females.

It wasn't until much later in human history, perhaps 35,000 years ago during the late Paleolithic era, that the elements of civilization began to appear which eventually resulted in the gross differentiation between men and women in terms of their physical and social roles. For example, with the discovery of the bow and arrow, man became a better and more efficient hunter. He no longer had to risk direct contact with his prey in order to kill it. This meant that the risks of the hunt were reduced and that fewer hunters were needed, allowing the clan to select those of its members most suited to the job. Females, because of their pregnancies, could not always be relied upon, so men assumed the responsibility of providing the band with fresh meat. Women were left behind with the children and the men went out into the field.

The skills needed for hunting were in many ways similar to those required to fight off enemies, so men became the warriors as well. Thus, men were the protectors and the providers and women assumed the responsibility of keeping the clan well supplied with infant soldiers and hunters. Motherhood became a specialized task. In this type of simple hunting society men had the most important jobs which meant that having male children was "better" than having female children. Since a woman could no longer attain status as a fighter and hunter, having a boy, especially a strong one who would grow up to be a fine hunter, conferred a vicarious status on the mother. This was, no doubt, the Stone Age equivalent of the "my son the doctor" syndrome.

Professor Alpenfels points out that along with the invention of the bow and arrow came the discovery of the needle with an eye. This simple tool enabled people to make better clothing from the skins of their prey. Since men were busy with the hunt, women were given the task of sewing. In a rudimentary form we can see that with the restrictions of motherhood came the tasks of sewing and cooking which we now think of as proper jobs for females. Perhaps more than any other invention, the bow and the needle laid the foundation for our present sexual division of labor. And it is this Stone Age thinking that still influences our social structure in the Space Age.

As mankind entered the Neolithic age and society changed from a hunting to an agrarian economy the men who had retained and developed their strength became farmers. In this more sheltered environment the weaker female children, who would have perished during the nomadic era, grew to adulthood and reproduced themselves. This eventually resulted in a down-breeding of the female stock so that today we find that women the world over are weaker and, on the average, two inches shorter than their men.

While the men worked the land women took on new jobs; pottery making, weaving cloth from plant fibers, and basic forms of housekeeping. While they performed these tasks, their babies were strapped to their backs or sleeping in nearby cradles. By the end of the Paleolithic era mother and infant had become inseparable.

The close association of women with children had only one basis in biological fact, females were capable of having babies and nursing them. There is nothing in the

4

psychophysical makeup of women that drives them or impels them to want children or to spend a good part of their adult lives raising them. If birth control methods had been available to those primitive people, no doubt some women, perhaps many, would have chosen to remain hunters and warriors rather than become cooks, sewers of clothing, and baby makers. But neither medical science nor society was capable of giving women that choice and it wasn't until the twentieth century that the option of having or not having children became available.

With the stabilization of society and the establishment of permanent homes, mankind was able to turn its attention from fighting for the bare essentials of life to founding a culture. Clans united to form tribes and tribes formed nations and each nation gradually assumed the characteristics of a socio-cultural pattern of human activities. Governments were established to regulate the relationship of people, laws were written to insure that these regulations were adhered to, and military forces were set up to provide internal and external security. For the most part women were left out of these new institutions because they had their job, motherhood. It became a man's world in which the males possessed the economic, governmental, legal, and religious power. Society was becoming stratified and the upper class was almost solely made up of men. The natural extension of this situation was for women to become little more than chattel whose only purpose was to provide men with children, preferably boys, to carry on the family name and to further the family fortune. Fertility was the paramount virtue of womanhood, far surpassing intelligence, creativity, or other talents. A woman who could not have children was considered worthless. In fact, among those societies that permitted men to divorce their wives, infertility was the major legal reason.

In addition to law and politics, religion played its part in promoting the idea that women *must* have children. There are many examples of this, but the most important one was the Cult of Mary that developed during the Middle Ages. Mary was the embodiment of the Ideal Woman. She was pure, sinless, and virgin, yet fertile enough to conceive the Son of God. Of course other women weren't quite able to conceive without sacrificing their virginity, but the example of Mary set the tone for female behavior. Pure beyond reproach, chaste except unto their husbands, and, most of all, mothers.

Thus, it became something of a religious duty for women to have children, especially male children to carry on the work of the world. The Madonna and Child epitomized womanhood and, to borrow a phrase, women adopted the Madonna Complex. Motherhood was a sacred institution and women, like the Holy Mother herself, were placed on pedestals and revered. However, they were revered as objects, not as people.

Being a madonna meant being protected from the distasteful aspects of life; the dog-eat-dog world of commerce, the intrigues and dishonesties of politics, and the vulgarities of the military. However, it is not at all certain that women wanted to be protected from these activities because they offered an excitement that was totally lacking in their daily duties. Women, in their role as wife and mother, had been glorified, but many found no glory in it. Betty Friedan, in her book *The Feminine Mystique*, describes this disappointment:

> The problem lay buried, unspoken, for many years in the minds of American women. It was a strange stirring, a sense of dissatisfaction, a yearning that women suffered in the middle of the twentieth century in the United States. Each suburban housewife struggled with it alone. As she made the beds, shopped for groceries, matched slipcover material, ate peanut-butter sandwiches with her children, chauffeured Cub Scouts and Brownies, lay beside her husband at night—she was afraid to ask even of herself the silent question—"Is this all?"*

We totally agree with Mrs. Friedan's description of the disillusionment that women feel with their role. However, we do not believe that this feeling began in the twentieth century nor that it is limited to the United States. More likely women have always sensed that theirs was a secondary and menial position and, if given the chance, they might have chosen other life-styles. But the socio-cultural pressures against this choice being granted were too great. The greatest pressure that forced women into accepting motherhood was a learned drive that they internalized almost from birth. It was the need to prove their womanhood by having children. It was the Myth of the Maternal Instinct.

The myth says that women innately want to have children because: A. Childbearing is the reason for their

---

* Betty Friedan, *The Feminine Mystique*, W. W. Norton Co. (New York, 1963) p. 11.

sex drive—the purpose of female sexuality is to reproduce the species; B. They are biologically designed to bear children and their minds are instinctively programmed to comply with their physiology; and C. Women have a natural need to nurture and love small children as a way of achieving personal fulfillment. Psychologists call this "care-giving behavior." This is what the mammaphiles would have women believe, and they did and still do. Unfortunately there is not a word of truth in it.

In the first place there is no instinctive purpose for the sex drive; people, not nature, give it a purpose. Sex can be used to express love, show affection, provide physical pleasure, *or* it can be used for procreation. Nature endowed women with the *capability* of having children but there is no innate drive which says they must use that capability. More than anything else it was the inability of women to prevent pregnancy which made them think that procreation was the reason for their sexual desires. In the past, birth control methods were either inadequate or totally lacking so when women made love they made babies. There was a pretty good correlation between copulation and procreation and that gave rise to some faulty cause-and-effect thinking: Sexuality creates a physical drive that must be satisfied. The satisfaction of that drive often causes pregnancy. Ergo, the reason for the drive was to become a mother.

This false logic put procreation in the same category as eating, drinking, sleeping, defecating, and breathing. The distinction that people failed to draw was that the latter drives have to be satisfied in order for people to go on living. They are *true* instincts. A woman, on the other hand, who fails to have children does not die. Consider the food intake instinct. People can diet, fast, or take appetite-reduction pills and ignore the hunger drive for a while, but they cannot go on indefinitely without food. To do so would cause death. The basic nature of an instinct is that it cannot be ignored for long without causing harm. But women can use some method of birth control each time they have intercourse and never suffer as a result. If procreation were an instinct, women would die from extended use of contraception. Since they do not, it is obvious that having babies is not a biological drive. Of course if all women did not have children, which is unlikely, the human species would die out. Instincts are not concerned with the species. They are concerned with the *individual member* of that species.

Another reason for the belief that having children was the innate purpose of sexuality, came from society's attitude that sex was base and dirty and that having children atoned for the sin of intercourse. Betty Rollin, in her excellent *Look Magazine* article, "Motherhood: Who Needs It?" said:

Originally, it was the word of God that got the ball rolling with "Be fruitful and multiply," a practical suggestion, since the only people around were Adam and Eve. But in no time, Super-moralists like St. Augustine changed the tone of the message: "Intercourse, even with one's legitimate wife is unlawful and wicked where the conception of the offspring is prevented," he, we assume, thundered. And the Roman Catholic position was thus cemented. So then and now, procreation took on a curious value among people who viewed (and view) the pleasures of sex as sinful. One could partake in the sinful pleasure, but feel vindicated by the ensuing birth. Motherhood cleaned up sex.*

Having children gave sexuality a spiritual purpose, a mystical motivation which provided all "good" people with a reason for indulging in intercourse besides sinful pleasure and enjoyment. The purpose of procreation then was to pay one's dues to morality.

Despite the faulty biological reasoning that procreation was instinctive and despite the religious notions about the purpose of intercourse, modern medical opinion offers no indication that sexuality must produce offspring. Dr. Clifford Allen, in his contribution to *The Encyclopedia of Sexual Behavior*, makes this clear in his discussion of the nature of the sexual instinct. Dr. Allen divides the sexual instinct into four parts—the stimulus, the strength of the urge, the mode of expression, and the sexual object**—none of which necessarily have anything to do with procreation.

The stimulus is whatever turns you on, whatever arouses the desire for sexual contact. For a man it could be the centerfold of a *Playboy Magazine*, for a women it could be the nearness of a handsome, exciting man. In these cases the arousal of sexual desire does not mean impregnating Miss November or becoming a mother.

* Betty Rollin, "Motherhood: Who Needs It?" *Look Magazine* (Vol. 34 No. 19) p. 15.
** Allen Clifford, "Sexual Perversions," *The Encyclopedia of Sexual Behavior*, Hawthorne Books, 2nd ed. (New York City, 1967) p. 803.

What it does mean is that a physical desire has been set into action and there is a need to satiate that desire. This is not dissimilar to Pavlov's dogs salivating when a bell was rung indicating that food was soon to be given to them. The beauty of a woman, the handsomeness of a man, *or* the desire to have children could be that bell. Procreation is only one of a number of stimuli that arouses the sexual instinct.

The strength of the sexual urge depends on a person's mental or physical state. A sailor who has been at sea for several months is psychologically and physically set to enjoy himself when his ship comes into port. When he seeks sexual companionship, his motive is strictly to experience the pleasure and release of a long built-up desire; he is not driven to intercourse by an overwhelming urge to be a father. In fact, it is probably the last thing he would want. By the same token, a woman whose husband has been on the road for two weeks wants to share the affection and fulfillment of intercourse she missed while he was away. And it is likely that she will use some type of contraception before she does so. Again, there is no procreation motive involved.

The Photographic Manual of Sexual Intercourse by L. R. O'Conner shows over a hundred ways to enjoy male-female intercourse, all of which are intended to increase pleasure, not the population. Then too, many people choose masturbation as their mode of expression. Over 90 percent of men have masturbated or do masturbate and many women choose masturbation as a frequent way of relieving sexual tension. If the instinctive purpose of sex was parenthood, fewer people would masturbate and those who did would masturbate less frequently. (In certain extreme cases, some people choose masturbation as their sole form of sexual expression.) Masturbation is not abnormal, it is simply an alternative form of erotic satisfaction as valid as heterosexual intercourse. If procreation were instinctive it would offer no alternatives. Breathing is instinctive and one has no choice but to inhale and exhale.

Finally, Dr. Allen talks about the sexual object; the man, woman, child, animal or thing selected to complete the sexual act. The sexual object can be a man if you are a woman or a woman if you are a man, but this choice does not necessarily mean babies; we are buying too many contraceptives to believe that. Furthermore, the great demand for abortion reform and the great number of women choosing legal or illegal abortions prove that even pregnancy touches off no instinctive urge to carry the fetus to maturity. Again, there are certain people who do not choose to have male-female intercourse. If the purpose of sex was babies then heterosexual intercourse would be the only means of satisfying the sexual drive. Everybody eats, sleeps, breathes, and defecates in more or less the same manner because they have no choice. But not everybody makes love the same way. Some choose to have babies, others choose not to; and when choice enters, instinct leaves.

One question almost invariably comes up with regard to the procreative nature of sexuality. That is: "If having offspring is not the instinctive motive for sex, why do animals seem to know that they must reproduce their own species through copulation?" This question assumes that there is some innate call of the wild within animals that makes them *want* to reproduce. *Wanting* puppies, or kittens, or lambs has not one iota of effect on animal sexuality. Dr. O. J. Miller, Professor of Human Genetics and Obstetrics and Gynecology at the Columbia College of Physicians and Surgeons, explains what does:

> The situation in almost all animals is quite different. That is, while males are capable of copulation most of the time—and of course in some species this is not true as males may only be capable of reproducing in certain seasons—the act of copulation is dependent upon the female being in heat, or estrus with a high level of estrogens.

Nature creates the estrous cycle, which brings about animal fertility at various times, so that they *can* procreate. This does not mean that they have the slightest understanding of the fact that copulation may result in pregnancy. Furthermore, experiments have demonstrated that female animals in estrous can experience relief from the physical discomforts of heat by artificial procedures which do not affect the well-being of the animal. If procreation were a physiological necessity the animals would have suffered as a result of these experiments.

In observing the mounting behavior of certain male animals, it is evident that procreation need not play a part in this behavior. Owners of male dogs will tell you how often they were embarrassed when their dogs locked onto the legs of guests and began copulative motions. If these dogs innately desired to procreate, instinct would have steered them away from human legs.

The Case Against Having Children

The second aspect of the myth of the maternal instinct, the assumption that women are biologically endowed with a desire to have children, is as false as the notion that procreation is the instinctive purpose of female sexuality. Society, not nature, programs women to desire motherhood. From their earliest years until the time they marry and have children, women are inundated with socio-cultural pressures that make motherhood appear to be a natural corollary of their femininity. This is done on an obvious level when girls are educated by their mothers in the ways of womanhood and on a subtle level through social cues that reinforce this learning process. Dr. Richard Radkin, a social psychiatrist practicing in New York City, explains this cueing-in process:

> Harry Harlow, the psychologist, was in San Antonio, Texas giving a lecture that my wife and I attended. The first thing he did was to put up a picture of an ugly infant, I mean a newborn monkey. It's kind of cadaverous. It doesn't have much meat on its bones. It's really honest-to-God ugly. The audience began to coo. There were a lot of college women, probably virgin, single, southwestern girls. The room sounded like a seaplane taking off, "oooh!" The room was roaring with coos. Now this is phony as hell. It's social pressure.

The coos these college women made served two purposes: In the first place they let everyone in the audience know that they loved children, even monkey children, which of course meant that they were "real women." Women are supposed to love babies. Any girl in the audience who made a sound of disgust when looking at the infant monkey would doubtless have been considered somewhat abnormal. This is a stimulus-response situation. Women are conditioned to respond with signs of affection when presented with a baby. The second purpose of the girls' affected response was to proselytize the religion of motherhood. Most of those college girls were looking forward to the day when they would become mothers and they wanted everyone to share their fervor.

The ways women are taught to desire children often resemble the techniques used by advertising agencies to sell people on the *need* for a product. Take mouthwash, for instance. People have managed to survive for a long time without using mouthwash and oral-medical studies show that it has negligible benefits, yet many individuals would not step out of the house without gargling. Madison Avenue has shown them on TV that non-garglers risk embarrassment, humiliation, and social rejection. Women face the same situation with motherhood. Social advertising—the opinions of parents, friends, and relatives —brainwashes women into believing that loving and being loved is the most important thing in their lives; that procreation always brings personal fulfillment; and that happy marriages are made in the maternity ward. Love, fulfillment, and happiness, are the gifts that children always bring; while pity and lack of purpose await the childless. When women have been conditioned to believe such concepts, there is little wonder why they desire to have babies. Motherhood is not something that women inherently want, it is a learned need. Of course, there are some women who do really wish to become mothers. The point is, the decision should be left up to the individual.

The campaign to make all women mothers begins at a very early age and the biggest promoters of motherhood are mothers themselves. There is a very complex socialization process which teaches little girls their *proper* role and it involves attitude shaping, personality structuring, and a myriad of other conditioning factors that eventually result in what we think of as normal female behavior. This is ridiculous; if it was normal mothers would not have to teach their daughters to act like women, they would do it naturally. The single best example of this socialization process is found in the games children play.

Overwhelming psychological research evidence supports the fact that one- and two-year-olds have no particular preference for one type of toy over another. Little boys and little girls show an equal interest in playing with dolls, trucks, and coloring books. But somewhat later in the pre-school years, a definite sex differentiation sets in. Boys tend to choose trucks while girls prefer dolls. The wrong assumption would be that they are beginning to show their innate sexual traits and that little girls, by selecting dolls, are exhibiting an incipient maternal drive. The fact of the matter is that social conditioning rather than sexual programing is responsible for little girls wanting to play with dolls, and this conditioning was carried out by their mothers. A little girl who shows a truck to her mother and asks how it works is cued into the idea that little girls should not concern themselves with trucks by her mother's total lack of knowledge and interest. On the other hand, when she shows her mother that she diapered her doll, momma smiles and says, "That doll is certainly lucky to have a mother like you. Some day you'll diaper a real baby of your own." The mother's pleased smile rewards the little girl for making an appropriate female response, one she will repeat again and again to get her mother's approval. In later life her desire for approval extends to society in general and she seeks motherhood as a way of finding approval among her friends, relatives, and neighbors who congratulate her on becoming pregnant and tell her about the fulfillments and joys of having children.

Modern technology is providing mothers with many aids for teaching their daughters lessons in maternity, foremost among them dolls that not only look like real babies, but *act* like them. There are dolls that wet their diapers, talk, and crawl. And now there is a doll that gets a tummy ache that little girls can cure with a miniature hot water bottle. The dolls with "life functions" provide little girls with the feeling of being grown-up because they can do almost the identical things their mothers do. The big problem with these dolls is that they show only the positive side of motherhood. In all fairness to womankind there should be a doll that requires so much attention that little girls cannot play with their friends as often as they would like or one that keeps them from going to parties or the movies because they cannot find a doll-sitter. However, this would be bad social advertising and it is doubtful that a Little Mary Monopolizer doll will ever be marketed. If little girls could see that there are pluses and minuses involved in motherhood, they might be motivated to weigh the relative satisfactions of childbearing against the relative satisfaction of other life-styles.

Doll play is by no means the only situation that directs girls toward motherhood, there are other forces at work and one of them is Option Limitation. Option Limitation is a technique used by mothers to make their daughters believe that women are only fit for the three C's—cooking, cleaning, and childbearing. The first phase of Operation Limited is designed to instill the so-called female traits of docility and subordination to men, thereby creating "perfect" wives. Our culture holds that women should never compete with men because a woman's place must be subordinate to her husband's. So strongly instilled is this idea that in reaction to women's lib an organization called M.O.M.—Men Our Masters—has been formed to actively picket for female slavery. These women believe there is a natural male superiority that females should not challenge. This type of thinking probably arises from situations like the one described by this young housewife and mother:

> When I think back I can remember the things that made me believe that being a girl wasn't as good as being a boy. For instance, I was always better at Ping-Pong than my brother and I beat him almost all the time. My mother would tell me to let Donald win more often because it wasn't right for a boy to be beaten by a girl. Boys were supposed to be better even if they weren't. Both my brother and I were good students but my parents always took a greater interest in Donald's education than mine. He would need all the schooling he could get so that he could find a good job. All I had to do was to find a husband, and that didn't

require being a genius. I never went to college. Donald did. My folks weren't rich and they figured it was a better investment sending a son to college than a daughter. I went to secretarial school and I hated every moment of it. It was dull, but I stuck it out. What made me stay was the thought that being a secretary was all a girl could or should be. Men were supposed to be the professionals and business executives and women were supposed to be their stenographers and typists. It's the same in business and marriage, women have to serve men. Men are on top and women are way down there somewhere at the bottom of the heap. I worked as a secretary until after I got married, but I quit when I became pregnant. Being a mother is better than being a secretary, but not much.

This young woman is typical of millions of women whose childhood experiences served to close their minds to alternative life-styles to marriage and motherhood. They were taught that women should not compete with men because doing so is unfeminine. There is nothing inherent in the genes of these women to make them think their place is in the home; the social conditioning process simply extinguished their ability to see themselves in roles that would bring them into competition with men. Many women believe they are unable to deal with men because they lack the drive, self-assurance, and the competitive spirit that males are supposed to have by virtue of their manhood. Psychologically speaking, what this amounts to is a mass inferiority complex carefully bred into women by their parents and the social structure. It is not uncommon to find women who believe that having children is the only way they can gain recognition and attain a feeling of accomplishment. They view motherhood as the one really important thing they can do well. "The only contribution I, as a woman, can make to society," said one mother of two children, "is to provide healthy, intelligent, capable children who will grow up to be responsible adults." This is a sad commentary because it suggests that women are only good for one thing, breeding. Above and beyond that, a woman's life really amounts to nothing.

The second phase of Option Limitation acts in such a way as to stifle the skills that women need to enter roles other than wife and mother. Girls and boys are selectively conditioned to be able to perform certain tasks well. Boys are oriented toward mechanics with erector sets, science with chemistry sets, and aggressive competitiveness with football and boxing. Girls are given dollhouses to learn decorating, toy tea service sets to make them good hostesses, and miniature cooking appliances to familiarize them with the kitchen. In elementary and high school boys are taught metal and wood work while girls learn home economics and sewing. Even on the college level, women are directed to take education courses because teaching is a proper female profession while men have a wide range of choices of major subjects. This second phase of Option Limitation serves as a back-up measure. Even if phase one failed to extinguish a woman's desire to compete with men, phase two makes it almost impossible because she lacks the necessary skills.

Option Limitation is a campaign for underachievement

carried out by mothers against their daughters and it serves two purposes. The first is obvious. Mothers feel they are doing the right thing teaching their daughters to be wives and mothers since that is what society will expect of them. The second reason is much less obvious. It is usually unconscious and is rooted in jealousy, fear, and anxiety.

The plain and simple truth is that most women resent other women who have achieved positions and status in the world outside the home. Polls and surveys show that the majority of women will not vote for a female political candidate, go to a woman doctor, or work for a lady executive. Women in high places threaten the average woman's self-image because their accomplishments make being a housewife and mother seem dull and unimportant by comparison. Their whole way of life becomes boring next to the exciting and important lives of successful career women. This of course will be denied by most women who outwardly feel that motherhood is still their most important task. We often hear the rationalization, "She may be a professional and earn lots of money, but she'll never know the fulfillment that comes with being a mother. I wouldn't trade my life with hers for all the money in the world." Reading between the lines though you can see an obvious attempt to build up their egos by expressing a false pity for the "misguided" woman who chose a career instead of motherhood. When you pity someone it tacitly means that yours is the enviable position while theirs is not quite so good.

Some women may suffer a certain feeling of anxiety when they think that their own daughters will accomplish things they themselves could not. Option Limitation is an attempt to keep that from happening. Nothing is more damaging to most women than having a professional daughter who has not the slightest inclination to become a wife and mother. The average woman would think she had failed terribly as a parent. She would have nothing in common with her daughter, she would feel slighted by her accomplishment, and she would never be able to face her friends on an equal footing if the daughter remained an old maid.

A woman with a Ph.D. in biology describes her experience with Option Limitation:

> My mother always said she was proud of my academic accomplishments, but I sensed something less than pride in her voice and attitude. Mother is from the old school and I'm certain she couldn't see the value of me, a woman, getting a Ph.D. in biology. I didn't date much in graduate school and my mother worried that I would never find a husband. It became almost a ritual with her to tell me about her friend's daughters who were happily married and had children. They were real women, I was an oddball. I remember the day I did become engaged, my mother went into a state of euphoria. She spent the entire evening on the telephone spreading the good news. She said she was happy for me, but she was much happier for herself. Her daughter had seen the light, her little girl had come home. Mother thought I would drop out of school and have children, but I told her that I was finishing my doctorate and that I intended to work after school. I

couldn't see any sense in putting in all those years and all that effort to cloister myself in a suburban baby factory. This disturbed my mother greatly and in despair and, I suspect, envy, she said, "Sometimes I wish you weren't so smart. Sometimes I wish you were a normal girl." And it's not only my mother who feels this way. Many of the girls I grew up with can't understand how I could enjoy my life in a laboratory surrounded by white mice and test tubes. They always try to convince me that I should have a child. It's almost as though there is a maternity conspiracy, like the Communist Party, trying to infiltrate my mind and make me Comrade Momma.

This woman managed to surmount the barriers of Option Limitation and find her own life. However, most women do not. They are indoctrinated with the idea that motherhood is the only salvation. To them, having children is the only alternative they can possibly select. It is, however, not their bodies, instincts, or hormones that tell them to have children, it is their minds, minds that were actively conditioned and brainwashed into believing that motherhood is the sole option a normal woman should choose.

The fact that women have reproductive systems is probably what makes us think motherhood is a natural female drive, a drive to comply with their physiology. Even Dr. Sigmund Freud thought so when he proclaimed, "Biology is destiny!"

The only thing that can be said about this brand of illogic is *phooey*! Such reasoning just does not hold water because it means that people should do only what they are biologically equipped for regardless of their intellectual, psychological, and creative potentials. For example, a man who weighs 200 pounds and has great strength and stamina is biologically equipped to be a construction worker. However, he also has a mathematically adroit mind, an interest in business law, and a talent for organization so he becomes an accountant. Is he in any way abnormal for choosing to work with his intellectual rather than his physical capabilities? Absolutely not! He is just exercising his freedom of choice and he has every right to do so. For women, on the other hand, it is a totally different story.

Just because females have the physical capability to reproduce we somehow feel that they *must* reproduce. All men do not have one purpose, why should all women? The answer of course is the maternal instinct, and this is no answer at all. There is nothing instinctual about a woman wanting a child and it is just as *natural* for her to be a childless business executive as it is for her to be a mother and housewife. To the "biology is destiny" people all that can be said is, biology, plus intelligence, plus personality, plus aptitude, equals alternatives. And motherhood is, or at least should be, one alternative among many.

Through the Myth of the Maternal Instinct, society has established the rule that all women want children and being an exception to that rule means being something of a social outcast. Even women who do not want children seldom admit to it. They profess to love children and say that the reason they are childless is because of illness, economic conditions, or other problems. They then go on to assure their listeners that as soon as the problem is cleared up they will become pregnant. Unfortunately these excuses cannot go on forever and social pressures can become so great that many women end up having children against their wishes. Dr. Henry Haberfeld, a psychiatrist on New York City's Mayor's Task Force on Child Abuse, tells of one such situation:

> I remember as a student I delivered a child to a 36-year-old woman. It was her first child although she had been married for many years and she expressed no joy in this. She was glad it was over, she wished she could have had an abortion. I asked her if she would like to see the child. She said no. Would she like to know if the child was all right? No. The next day I asked her how she felt about things. She said she didn't want the child but that she was stuck with it. I remember this. It's been fifteen years, but I still shudder to think of what's happened to that child.

The usual response to examples like this is that the woman in question is a monster, an abnormal creature. But it is not her instincts that are deficient. She simply never learned to want children and the sad thing is that she went ahead and got pregnant anyway. Very likely she felt that as a woman she *must* have children but then, later in her pregnancy, discovered this was not true. Of course then it was too late.

Unfortunately this case is not exceptional. A recent survey shows that approximately 750,000 unwanted children are born each year in the United States. This does not mean there are 750,000 instinctually deficient mothers; what it does indicate is that three quarters of a million women should have chosen alternatives to motherhood or requested abortions. And in so doing they would have spared both themselves and their unwanted children an untold amount of grief, unhappiness, frustration, and emotional conflict. No woman *must* have a child if the birth of that child holds such unfortunate consequences.

The third aspect of the maternal instinct myth says that women have an inborn desire to care for, feed, and nurture their children. If this were true it would mean that women the world over would share a common need to express care-giving behavior to their babies. This is not the case because anthropological evidence indicates that in many cultures women play only a minor role in raising their children. Professor Alpenfels explains that there are four distinct ways in which children may be cared for— by the mother, the grandparents, by older siblings, or by the father. So-called maternal behavior in women may seem perfectly natural to us, but other cultures may think caring for babies is very unfeminine because it is a man's job.

In arguing against the instinctive nature of female care-giving behavior one often encounters the retort, "If caring for a loving offspring is not innate, how do you explain the fact that animal mothers feed and protect their young? Certainly they are not influenced by cultural patterns and concepts of proper behavior." Granted that animals, dogs for example, are not socially conditioned to care for their puppies, but neither are they motivated by mother love. Something else directs dogs to express maternal behavior. John Paul Scott, in his book *Animal Behavior*, explains what that something is:

> A mother dog whose pups have been taken away becomes very uneasy and restless as the mammary glands become filled with milk; and this excitement can apparently be considerably reduced by applying irritating substances which inhibit the flow of milk. In the case of milk secretion we have a definite physiological change which can act as a nervous stimulus.*

If anything, selfishness, not affection, is the reason for a mother dog keeping her pups safe and sound. During and after pregnancy she becomes lactiferous, milk-producing, and the milk collecting in her mammaries is a source of discomfort. When her pups nurse and draw out the milk, she experiences relief. It is not the puppies themselves that a mother dog becomes attached to, it is their ability to make her feel better that makes her want them around.

In some of the higher species of mammals, notably the primates, learning *does* play the key role in maternal behavior. This is proven through an experiment carried out by Seay, Alexander, and Harlow.

The subjects of this experiment were socially deprived rhesus monkeys who had been taken from their mothers at birth and raised in isolation from other monkeys. When these "motherless monkeys" grew to adulthood, they were mated and when they gave birth, showed some very unmotherlike behavior:

* John Paul Scott, *Animal Behavior*, University of Chicago Press (Chicago, 1958), p. 84.

> All seven of the MM (motherless mothers) monkeys
> were totally inadequate mothers and their infants pre-
> sumably would have died without intervention and
> feeding by staff members. Initially the MM monkeys
> tended to ignore or withdraw from their babies. . . .
> Later the motherless mothers were so cruel that for
> varying periods of time we feared for their infants'
> lives and in the case of two other MMs, their infants
> died shortly after forced maternal separation.*

If these socially deprived monkeys had had the chance
to experience mothering themselves, or if they had seen
other female monkeys caring for their young, they would
have been more adequate mothers. Being denied these
opportunities, the MM monkeys had no cues as to the
proper behavior to exhibit when their own infants
appeared. The same thing goes for human mothers. A
girl whose own mother was deficient in her maternal
behavior will herself probably be an inadequate mother
because she has no model to follow. Tender loving care
is not something women give instinctively, they must
first observe it. There is nothing spiritual, mystical, or
genetically inherited in the female makeup that impels
women to nurture and love their babies, it is simply a
case of mother see, mother do.

Care and concern for the well-being of infants is so
socially promoted that mothers who do not really love
their children experience strong feelings of guilt. This
guilt is responsible for a phenomenon that psychologists

* B. Seay, B. Alexander, and H. Harlow, "Maternal Behavior
of Socially Deprived Monkeys," *Journal of Abnormal and Social
Psychology* (1964, vol. 66 no. 4), p. 353.

call maternal overprotection which is a sublimation of maternal rejection. Overprotective mothers feel they have to prove to themselves, their family, and society, that they love their children, so they become super mothers. They call in the doctor if the child shows the slightest sign of a sniffle, they carefully screen their children's friends lest they should fall prey to bad influences, and they fill their children's mouths with enormous quantities of food to make certain they are well nourished. But this is a phony concern and it is more for show than for the well-being of the child.

At the other end of the scale there are rejecting mothers who do not conceal their feelings. These women are responsible for the infant abandonment and battered child cases we so often hear about. If loving maternal concern for children was instinctual there would be no babies left in trash cans or young children beaten almost to the point of death—and sometimes beyond.

Unlike some myths that have a determinable basis of fact, the Myth of the Maternal Instinct is a complete fabrication resting on three totally incorrect premises. Yet it has managed to endure for centuries. If the myth was so far off base, why did it last so long and why wasn't it exploded years ago? The answer is that there were vested interests that profited from making women believe that they had no alternative but to become mothers. These were, and still are, the economy, society, and women themselves.

Historically we have always believed that the wheels of the economy moved best when amply oiled by a large and growing population. In the days of the simple agricultural economy, large families meant more hands to work the fields, harvest the crops, and tend the animals. Children, especially male children, were capital assets and a woman's major value was her fertility. When the Industrial Revolution brought people from the farms to the factories an even larger pool of manpower was required to keep the mills running and to create increased markets for mass-produced goods. Businessmen, who controlled society, saw an inevitable correlation between higher population figures and higher profit figures and they, through their wealth and political power, promoted the ideal of the large family. This male domination of the right of women to bear or not to bear children continues today. There is ample evidence of this among the male legislators who vote down abortion reform. While they claim their motives are strictly humanitarian, the truth is that they are still locked into the idea that an increasing population equals a thriving economy. Wayne H. Davis, a professor of biological sciences at the University of Kentucky, believes that this type of thinking is disastrous to both the economy and society:

Our economy is based upon the Keynesian concept of a continued growth in population and productivity. It worked in an underpopulated nation with excess resources. It could continue to work only if the earth and its resources were expanding at an annual rate of 4 to 5 percent. Yet neither the number of cars, the economy, the human population, nor anything else can expand indefinitely at an exponential rate in a finite world. We must face this fact *now*. The crisis is here. . . .

A civilization is comparable to a living organism. Its longevity is a function of its metabolism. The higher the metabolism (affluence) the shorter the life. Keynesian economics have allowed us an affluent but short lived life span. We have now run our course.*

The evidence is all around us. We are using up our natural resources at a faster rate than science and technology can provide us with acceptable synthetic substitutes. Someday there will be nothing left to purchase just as there will be no place to live because the last parcel of land has been used for the last house. As Representative Morris E. Udall of Arizona puts it, there will be "standing room only on Spaceship Earth." For the sake of generations to come, the Myth of the Maternal Instinct must be laid to rest because it is economically unfeasible. The cost of telling all women they *must* have children is too dear.

Society is a collective of individuals who banded together for their mutual benefit and who eventually created various social institutions which they came to revere and worship. Religion is one such institution and national states are another. It is inevitable that the institutions of society become more important than the people who created them and this leads to the assertion that although people die, society must live. It is through their

* Wayne H. Davis, "Over Populated America," *The New Republic* (Jan. 10, 1970), pp 14-15.

culture that a people achieve a kind of immortality. Whether or not this is as important or as necessary as people make it out to be is open for debate. The world was probably a more peaceful and a more beautiful place before man and his civilizations put in their appearance. There are many who believe that through his destructiveness, his cruelty, and his carelessness, man has given up his right to continue living in a world that he is slowly destroying. But let us assume that, for whatever reasons, society and the human species must continue and that means that women *must* have babies. There is still no reason for all women to have children nor do those women who choose to become mothers have to have lots of children. In fact, ecologists say that if society wishes to continue it must strive for a lower birthrate. Therefore, women must be taken off the maternity merry-go-round and offered alternative life-styles. They must be made to feel that motherhood is not a compulsory social duty. The question now remains, how many children do we need to reproduce the species in sufficient numbers to maintain our society? There are no hard and fast guidelines, although there are many valid opinions. Some individuals and organizations like Zero Population Growth which seeks to equalize the birth rate with the death rate, believe that families should have no more than two children to replace the parents. Others, like Wayne H. Davis, believe that even two may be too many:

American women average slightly over three children each. According to the *Population Bulletin*, if we reduced this number to 2.5 there would still be 330 million people at the end of the century. And even if we reduced this to 1.5 we would still have 57 million more people in the year 2000 than we have now.*

This means that if we cut the size of our average family in half, or if half the women in America stopped having children while the rest had three, our nation would still have a net population increase of 57 million. Such statistics make it plain that women can seriously think about alternatives to motherhood without destroying the human species. The time has now come for the Myth of the Maternal Instinct to be changed to the "Fact of the Maternal Alternative" which would tell women there are valuable contributions that they can make to society other than children.

The social and economic interests that promote the Myth of the Maternal Instinct could not possibly have done so for these thousands of years unless they were aided and abetted by women themselves. It was ultimately the need that women had for the myth that guaranteed its long life. Killing the myth means attacking the need that nourishes it and this is difficult, because to a large extent it is rooted in a woman's natural desire to avoid depersonalization.

Our social structure depersonalizes women by assuming that they all have an unqualified interest in child care. This strips away their individuality and forces over 50 percent of our population to join a Sisterhood of Sameness. The Myth of the Maternal Instinct at least provides women with the rationalization that their role is inevita-

* Ibid., p. 15.

ble. If motherhood is instinctual, if women are biologically destined to have children, then there is no sense in feeling dissatisfied with being a mother because there is no alternative. It is only when alternatives do appear that women fully realize the boring nature of their social position. A good example of this occurred after World War II.

When American men took up arms in Europe their women were called to fill the vacancies in the factories, the mills, and offices. To their amazement women found they were able to do "men's work" as well as men, and that included heavy construction-line jobs. Rosie the Riveter was not an abnormal lesbian in laborer's overalls, she was the attractive feminine girl-next-door who was helping to save her nation. Women found new identities in the world outside the home and they realized they could produce work that was worth a weekly paycheck. (Incidentally, many women who now enter the business world often are quite willing to accept low salaries. Having done free housework all their lives, they feel that whatever they are paid is probably more than they are worth. This is one of the big reasons for the salary differential between males and females doing the same work. Women have not had the chance to learn to ask for more than is offered to them.) The identity of being a wage earner and the supporter of a family was, to many women, a psychological shot in the arm. It was conclusive proof that they were good for more than feeding children and scrubbing floors.

This came to an abrupt halt when the soldiers returned. The economy no longer needed the women and they were packed off to their kitchens and nurseries. But the housewives did not forget the variety, fulfillment, challenge, and self-actualization of working outside the home. For many, motherhood and wifehood had lost its previous meaning and what they needed was something to revitalize their "female desire" to be housewives and mothers. So, the Myth of the Maternal Instinct, which had seemed totally irrelevant during the war, was dusted off and updated. The need to have children became the need for natural childbirth. Anesthetized childbirth was too easy and anything easy is unimportant. The need to nurture children became the need to breast-feed them. This gave Momma a feeling that she could not be replaced by a sterilized bottle. In addition, women read the thousands of books and articles that told them how to be better mothers, mothers who could take a more meaningful role in the lives of their children.

Simply defined, selfishness means being concerned mainly with one's self. It further means that selfish people are exploitative, they use others to promote their own best interests. Many women, perhaps even the majority, tend to have children for selfish reasons because they use their children as vehicles to achieve the things they want out of life but are unable to attain.

Our culture places a great premium on status, position, and possession. Keeping up with the Jones family is an old tradition. Society makes it possible for men to achieve status and recognition through their jobs. Any man who puts out even a moderate amount of effort will reap some kind of reward. For women this is not so. Women cannot earn a status position, they must have it conferred upon them by others. Marriage does this. When a woman marries she becomes so-and-so's wife and she assumes whatever prestige her husband has. Women lead a vicarious life basking in the reflected glory of their husbands' achievements. They also achieve status through their children.

Having children does a lot for a woman. First, it gives her the identity of being someone's mother. If her children are attractive, smart, or well-mannered, Momma receives compliments that add to her own prestige. If her children aren't too smart or if they cause trouble, she has worries and problems that she can complain about. Either way, a woman can attract some sort of attention through her offspring.

Children provide women with security. Having children reduces the likelihood of divorce, or so they think, and women use their children as a way of holding onto their husbands. And even if the marriage does break up, the woman will always have her children to cling to.

A mother can also use her baby as a way of achieving power. Being dominated by men, women have a need to impose their wills on someone less strong than themselves. Having a child to order about permits a woman to exert some dominance.

Women may have children so that they share in their child's accomplishments in later life. A mother can look forward to her son becoming a successful professional or her daughter marrying a successful professional and this gives her something to tell her friends about thereby achieving a status position among them.

These, and the other many motives discussed in the

next chapter, are selfish reasons for desiring motherhood. But most women will not admit to them. Indeed, selfishness and motherhood are, according to our way of thinking, mutually exclusive. There is nothing worse than a selfish mother, a mother who uses her child. This is where the Myth of the Maternal Instinct comes in. Women who want children for exploitative reasons can offer the myth as their reason for becoming mothers. Since motherhood is instinctual and inescapable, who can blame a woman for wanting a child? The Myth of the Maternal Instinct places a pleasant veneer over a conscience made uneasy by pinpricks of selfishness.

II

The Wrong Reasons for Motherhood

The case against having children in no way means that everyone should stop having children. What it *does* mean is that women and men should carefully analyze their motives for parenthood with the intention of determining: A. if their desire to have children honestly reflects their own wishes or if it represents a sense of expectation or compulsion arising from socio-cultural pressures; B. if, already being parents, the birth of another child is truly necessary or advisable in terms of the best interests of their existing families and society in general; and C. if their motives for seeking parenthood are altruistic or selfish.

In the previous chapter we exploded the single greatest social and cultural force that impels women toward motherhood, the Myth of the Maternal Instinct. In a later chapter we will talk in some detail about the many negative aspects of having large families, but for now let's zero in on the faulty psychological and emotional motives for parenthood, or, more specifically, the wrong reasons for motherhood.

Any woman who becomes pregnant with the hope that her child will give her something she lacks, or do something for her that she has not been able to do for herself, is being selfish. No baby should be born having to fulfill an obligation in order to win complete acceptance from its mother. Every child should be wanted for himself, not for what he symbolically represents. In other words, many babies are brought into the world with strings attached to their acceptance. "Rescue my marriage and I'll love you." "Give me an identity and we'll get along just fine." "Grow up to be someone special and I'll be proud of you." Though many women may be unwilling to admit these egotistic and selfish reasons for motherhood to themselves, psychologists, psychiatrists, and sociologists, have found them to be strongly operant motives in the decision to bear children. And the thing that makes them so wrong is the disastrous consequences that may result for the mother and the child if the child fails to measure up to its mother's great expectations.

A woman who is gambling on the possibility that becoming a mother will solve certain personal problems may find that by having a child she is compounding her troubles. If having a child isn't the answer then she not only has her original difficulty to overcome but also the responsibility for a child she doesn't truly want. The time and effort that raising a child requires may prevent her from ever overcoming whatever it was that drove her to maternity. As for the child who doesn't fulfill his mother's selfish motives, he may experience rejection, hostility, or even worse, physical abuse, neglect, or abandonment, all because he couldn't do a job he didn't know he was hired to do.

There are many wrong reasons for motherhood, but the following represent the ones most frequently recognized by professionals in the field of parent-child relations.

"My child will be somebody."

In his article "Clinical Notes on Motives of Reproduction," Dr. Frederick Wyatt says that identification—the psychological dynamism used by individuals to find status and self-identity by associating themselves with the achievements of others—is used more often by women than by men.* This is understandable. All of us, male and female, are conditioned to want status and recognition, but as a rule only the males are actually able to go out and create status positions. For the most part women have been, and still are, denied access to the top positions in business, the professions, and public life. The best most women can hope for is secondhand recognition by associating themselves with their husbands' accomplishments. A wife's only share in her husband's status role is the idea that she was in some way responsible for helping him get where he is. The wife who worked so that her husband could attend medical school, the woman whose talents as a hostess helped her husband impress an important client, and the political candidate's wife whose charm

* Fredrick Wyatt, "Clinical Notes on Motives of Reproduction," *Journal of Social Issues* (1967, vol. 23, no. 4), p. 51.

helped her husband win an election, all smile proudly when someone compliments them by saying, "Behind every great man there's a good woman." This is the crumb of glory with which they must be content.

Then again, not every woman marries a man who has enough status to share. He may be respected as an honest working man and a good provider, but that doesn't say anything for his wife. In such cases many women look to childbearing as a way of getting recognition. Some even have children with the expressed purpose of pushing them to positions of importance for which they will eventually be able to take credit. "My son the doctor. If it weren't for me, he'd never even have gotten through college." No doubt there are many people who have gone on to great things because of their mothers' need for recognition, but often these children pay a price for satisfying their mothers' egos. A child psychiatriast, practicing in an upper-middle-class New York suburb, tells what that price is:

It's almost unimaginable how many children—young kids in elementary school—I see in my office who seem to have the weight of the world on their shoulders. They're nervous, anxious—like scaled-down models of businessmen worried about some big deal that could fall through at any moment . . . they're afraid of not doing well on a math test or a spelling test because they don't want to disappoint their mothers. . . . I'm working with one little boy—he's eight years old—who won't bring home a test paper with less than ninety percent. He recopies his tests, fills in the right answers, and gives himself a higher grade. His mother is worried about his being dishonest. What she should be worried about is the overcompetitiveness, fear of failure, and anxiety over disappointing his mother that she's instilled in the child. And this boy isn't an isolated case. Many mothers tell me that they stress excellence in school because education is the only way their children may make something out of themselves. They're convinced that they only want the best for their kids. Bullshit! I'll tell you what they want. They want the best for themselves. . . . At report card time Mrs. Jones will call Mrs. Smith to find out how Mrs. Smith's child did. If he didn't get as good grades as Mrs. Jones's child, she has something to boast about. . . . These mothers judge their children's worth by relative standards: Better than Johnny but not as good as Bobby. Their children are not individuals who are loved and accepted for their good points as well as their bad points, they're yardsticks that their mothers can use to measure their motherly capabilities. A high achiever means "I'm a good mother" and that means higher status among her friends. A low achiever means the opposite, so the child gets pushed a little harder. He becomes a nervous wreck and his only opinion of himself is based on his success or failure in school. . . .

. . . in this community every woman has attained the Great American Dream. The expensive house, the new car, a wardrobe full of the best clothes, and a husband with a good job or profession. Nobody can impress anyone else with their wealth, so a woman has to look elsewhere to find status. So she uses her kids. Women use their children to compete with other women. In elementary school it may be report card grades, later on it may be getting the child into a prestige college and eventually into a professional school . . . but it does the child no good and it does the mother no good because she still has done nothing for herself. It would be a lot better if these mothers left their children alone and did something for themselves to achieve a feeling of accomplishment. If these women got some recognition outside the home they wouldn't feel compelled to force their kids to achieve for them. . . .

This psychologist is echoing the cry of the women's liberation movement that calls for more opportunities for women for self-expression and the chance to create their own status positions which will give them a feeling of accomplishment. Imagine what the results would be if women stopped pushing their children and redirected some of that incredible drive and determination toward their own careers or educations. Such a change may be some time in coming. Until then, identification will continue to be an important defense mechanism for women. Mothers will continue insisting that all the self-sacrifice and effort they expend in their children's behalf is purely altruistic and intended for their children's best interests. It's not. When a mother says, "I want my child to be somebody," she may really be saying, "*I* want to be somebody."

"Having a child will save my marriage."
The increasing incidence of divorce in our country has

made it easier for unhappy couples to end their marriages without being stigmatized by society. But even this liberalization does not prevent many women from experiencing emotional panic when confronted with the possibility of their marriages dissolving. Frequently they will try almost anything to regain their husbands' affection or, failing that, to at least insure the continuation of the marriage. And unfortunately many of them see childbearing as a way of forcing their husbands to remain with them. "With children," these wives calculate, "my husband will not leave me. His sense of duty and responsibility will keep him at home." Often their calculations are quite accurate. Said one young husband:

> I knew after the first two years that the marriage had no chance of working. . . . The excitement of the first year really distracted us from each other. We were busy furnishing the apartment . . . I had started a new job . . . Susan was involved with the novelty of marriage. . . . But when that passed it wasn't replaced by anything. The excitement died and then we started to become more aware of each other . . . we didn't grow toward each other, we grew away from each other. . . . There were petty arguments over nothing, family problems, the works. I don't have to spell it out. It was just a mistake. The whole marriage was a mistake. . . . Neither of us spoke about divorce, but we both knew it was inevitable. Maybe if we did talk it out and decide to end the marriage we would have both been better off. . . . Then Susan became pregnant. I felt as though the walls were closing in on me. I wanted out, but now

there was no chance. In good conscience I couldn't leave. . . . A child should grow up with a father and mother in the house . . . I guess when my son's old enough to understand that his mother and father don't get along, then we'll get a divorce. . . . It's terrible living this way, but it's the only way. It's for the baby's good.

This father, for all his noble intentions, is probably doing the wrong thing. Numerous psychological studies clearly show that the tensions, anxieties, and hostilities existing between incompatible parents are far more detrimental to a child's mental health than living in a home with only one parent. Often it is not the child's best interests that parents are truly concerned with. The following interview excerpt illustrates the selfish intent a woman may exhibit when faced with the prospect of divorce:

> . . . the three month trial separation convinced me that being married, even with the fights and aggravation, was a lot better than being single. . . . All my friends were married and they just stopped calling me. I'm sure it was nothing personal, it's just that when you're single you're odd man out . . . And I didn't especially relish the idea of going to places to meet men. When you're young you have the patience for playing games, but I just couldn't see myself going through all the effort and hassle of dressing up, going alone to a dance or a singles' bar, and fighting my way through an army of creeps just to find one halfway decent guy . . . When we got back together, it seemed as though

things would work out and we both thought that having a child would make our marriage really work.
We'd have something in common, something to focus
our attention on. . . . We still don't have a great marriage, a lot of the old problems are still there. But, for
better or worse, we're still together.

It is obvious that this woman is using her child as a
shield against divorce which, despite her unhappy marriage, she considers to be the greater of two evils. She is
making no personal attempt to improve the quality of her
marriage, that burden has been placed on her baby. This
probably will not work, and Dr. Rebecca Liswood, physician, marriage counselor, and author of many books and
articles on marital relations, explains why:

Those couples, too immature to make a good adjustment to each other, are too immature to have children
and they have children for the wrong reasons. They
will say, "I'm having a child because our marriage is
very bad and the child will cement the marriage."
Actually having a baby is the worst thing they can do
because they are adding additional problems that will
guarantee the fact that they will never get along. A
little tiny child cannot bring them closer together
because that infant needs love and attention, love and
attention a couple must take away from each other in
order to give to that child. This makes things worse.
No couple has the right to bring a child into a marriage that isn't functioning. They would be far better
off either improving the marriage or getting divorced
before children are involved.

In many cases women who have had children in an attempt to keep their marriages from breaking up find that they did nothing but prolong the inevitable. The divorce happens anyway. Then with the husband gone many of these women rely so heavily on their child for love, affection, and certain narcissistic ego needs, that the child becomes unable to form meaningful relations with friends or with people of the opposite sex. A kind of psychological symbiosis occurs. The mother satisfies her affectional needs solely from her child, and the child, who is blocked from developing attachments outside the home, comes to view his mother as his sole source of emotional fulfillment. This is the most obvious example of maternal selfishness. The mother uses the child without any regard for his own psychological and social needs. In some cases the use of children to fulfill a woman's affectional need may become a motive for motherhood without the actual threat of divorce being present. Women, seeing that the institution of marriage is no longer as stable as it once was, may opt for motherhood in anticipation of the possibility of divorce. "A husband's affections can change," they say to themselves, "but a child will always love its mother." Thus, motherhood becomes a kind of love insurance. By investing in a pregnancy when the marriage is going well, a wife can assure herself of someone to love and be loved by in the eventuality that her husband leaves her either by divorce or death.

At the other extreme, a child who was conceived to preserve a marriage that subsequently dissolves may be totally rejected by his mother. She may even decide that

47

the baby was responsible for the divorce, telling herself that the child stole her husband's love and affection. Then too, a mother may resent her child because he reminds her of the man who rejected her. Some divorced women feel their children are obstacles in finding a new husband. They believe that a man will not want to take on the responsibility of another man's child.

In any of these eventualities, the child can suffer greatly. He may think that he was responsible for his parents' divorce or develop such hostility toward his mother that he has trouble relating to society in general. These, and a variety of other emotional problems resulting from maternal rejection can totally distort a child's personality.

For women and, for that matter, men considering having children in an attempt to salvage their marriages, Dr. Liswood offers these valuable words of advice:

> A mother owes her children a certain amount of consideration. She should only bring a child into a relationship where there is fun and laughter and, above all, a sincere consideration and respect that she and her husband have for each other. A child should never be brought into an environment filled with emotional turmoil.

"I had an unhappy childhood. My child won't."

People who suffer long and severe periods of hardship often try to imbue their suffering with a sense of purpose. It is difficult for an individual to reconcile himself to the fact that the slings and arrows of outrageous fortune are often unaimed and tend to strike arbitrarily. To accept this is to accept personal insignificance. If a person's life is filled with suffering and if there is no meaning in that suffering then there is no meaning in their lives. Many women try to justify their past unhappiness by becoming a mother. Psychiatrist Dr. Henry Haberfeld explains how this can happen:

> There are many women who were unhappy as children. They may have had severe difficulties with siblings or perhaps their parents were neglectful or abusive. So they say to themselves, "I was so unhappy as a child that when I have a child I'm going to do the best I possibly can." That determination was formed out of their life experiences, and their purpose is to assure themselves that their own suffering wasn't wasted.

The motive, then, for becoming mothers is an attempt on the part of these women to balance out their unhappiness against a greater good. "The miserable treatment I received as a child was to show me how *not* to treat my own children," these women may rationalize. Being good mothers becomes the purpose for their lives, the objective they suffered so long to achieve.

On another level, women with difficult childhoods may desire motherhood as an attempt to prove to themselves that they can be adequate parents despite the inadequacies of their own mothers. Writes Dr. Mark Flapan:

> . . . a woman who considers her mother to have been inadequate and unfulfilled in motherhood may look

forward to childbearing as a means of demonstrating her ability to be a good mother in comparison to her own mother. In the role of mother, she may be determined to create a family life different from that she experienced as a child and establish a more satisfying relationship with her children than the one she had with her own mother. She may want to prevent her children from having the kind of unhappy childhood she experienced, and wish to provide them with the experiences she missed as a child.*

Dr. Flapan suggests another possible motive for motherhood; an opportunity for women who have had unsatisfactory childhoods to create a Heaven on Earth for their own offspring so that they, the mothers, can vicariously share in the joys they were denied.

No one can argue with a mother who wants to create a constructive and enjoyable environment for her child provided that her intentions are solely to promote the child's well-being. However, a woman seeking motherhood in an attempt to justify her childhood suffering, or to prove herself a better parent than her own mother, or perhaps to experience a satisfactory childhood through her children is apt to be a very self-demanding parent whose ego needs can only be satisfied by being a *perfect* mother, and that is an impossibility. Moreover, the need for perfection is a selfish need concerned only with providing the mother with something she feels is missing in

* Mark Flapan, "A Paradigm for the Analysis of Childbearing Motivations of Married Women Prior to Birth of the First Child," *American Journal of Orthopsychiatry* (1969, vol. 39, no. 3), p. 410.

her life. If she fails in achieving this, she may well end up making her child as unhappy as she herself was in the past.

"Having a child will make me an adult."

Broadly speaking, there are four kinds of maturity—physical, intellectual, social, and psychological. Physical maturity simply means the development of the bodily and organic characteristics of an adult. Intellectual maturity may be understood as the ability to learn and reason. Girls tend to grow up physically and intellectually more rapidly than boys during middle childhood, but boys catch up during adolescence. Social maturity is a legal concept that gives people certain rights and obligations at various age levels. There is a legal age at which people are considered old enough to marry without their parents' consent, or enter into binding contractual agreement, or exercise their right to vote. These are more or less the same for both sexes. The big difference between male and female maturity is psychological. Being an adult in the psychological sense means going from dependence to independence; progressing from nonaccountability for one's behavior to total personal responsibility, giving up "other-directedness" and assuming self-direction. And this is where society separates the men from the women. Males are taught a sense of responsibility, an attitude of self-determination, an ability to make decisions, and a capability of providing for themselves and their families. Women are taught to find husbands who will take care of them. Women are trained for marriage and the institution of marriage, in our socio-cultural tradition, is in essence a

51

transfer of a woman's dependence from her parents to her husband. A housewife-turned-career-woman puts it this way:

> . . . and after about a year of marriage I realized how absurd the whole concept of the man and wife relationship was. For the wife it's really a kind of regression. I mean there I was, 25 years old, a college graduate, two and a half years of business experience under my belt and I had to depend on my husband to give me an allowance. Sure, you can euphemize it and call it a household budget, but it's still an allowance just the same. . . . And if I wanted to buy a coat or a dress I had to ask Harry for the money; I went through that when I was ten years old. Don't misunderstand me, Harry is a great guy and he's very generous, but I didn't marry him so that he could become a father substitute. . . . I know there are many women who want their husbands to make all the decisions and dominate their lives. My feeling is that they just haven't grown up. They're afraid to face the real world. They need someone to protect and guide them.
>
> . . . as I said, I tried the housewife bit for a year, then I went back to work. I like the feeling of making my own money, of having some independence. . . . It took Harry a little while to get used to this, but now he agrees it's for the best. He doesn't have to shoulder all the burdens because we can work things out together.

What this lady is talking about is a man-woman relationship as opposed to a man-wife relationship, and the difference is not insignificant. Man-wife marriage means male domination and female subordination whereas a man-woman relationship indicates a partnership of equals.

For the most part women tend to desire male domination. But while they are willing to be dependent on their husbands they do need *some* sense of responsibility as an indication of their adulthood. Childbearing provides this. Being a mother, for some women, is synonymous with being an adult because the role of mother implies having a responsibility for someone else's well-being. And, perhaps more important, it means having power.

Maturity and immaturity are relative conditions often differentiated by degrees of authority. Children are virtually powerless and they are subject to the authority of their parents. Thus children, boys as well as girls, grow up aspiring toward parenthood as a way of getting power and thereby having evidence of their maturity. In time this becomes less important for men because they can satisfy their egos in other ways than dominating children. They attain authority on their jobs, they have subordinates or employees whose work they can direct, or they marry and dominate their wives. Women do not have these outlets so they have children whose lives *they* can dominate. In effect, they create their own subordinates and confer upon themselves an illusion of maturity. And it *is* an illusion because having children makes them *seem* like adults when, in reality, they themselves are in a childlike subordinate position in relation to their husbands.

Like the other wrong reasons for having children, this motive is both selfish and exploitative. Women who become mothers so that they can have a feeling of responsibility are asking their children to help them grow up. In the final analysis their interest is not in their children, but what they stand for. Symbolically, motherhood means maturity.

"Having a child will prove I'm a sexually mature woman."

Probably the most important step in an individual's development of an ego identity is the establishment of a sexual identity. When young children begin to realize they are either boys or girls they start adopting the socially approved thought and behavior patterns that ultimately direct them to the roles they will play as adults. It is the association that children make between themselves and their sex group that lays the foundation for their personalities. But if anything happens to undermine this foundation, if a child is not completely convinced of its maleness or femaleness, then the development of a healthy adult personality is impeded. For example, our culture says that a man should have a dominant and assertive personality, but there are many men who have the so-called female traits of docility or submissiveness. These men may feel unmasculine or castrated, so in order to prove their manhood they overcompensate by being excessively domineering with their wives and children. By doing this they are attempting to alleviate the threat to their egos caused by their sexual uncertainty. Women do the same thing. If a girl grows up feeling unfeminine, she may do many things to convince herself she is a woman and having children is one of them. Since becoming pregnant and bearing children are things that only women can do, motherhood is, for some women, a way of overcoming the doubts they have about their sexual adequacy. Mr. Ira Neiger of Planned Parenthood of New York City is not unfamiliar with this faulty motive for childbearing:

> Some women equate pregnancy and childbearing with their femininity and the social role they are expected to play. Certain women, many of them young—although older women may feel the same way—are not particularly sure of their sexuality and often getting pregnant is an important thing for them to do so that they can prove their femininity.

On the whole, women who have doubts concerning their sexual identity are reacting to their parents and their social milieu. A girl whose father always wanted a boy and treats her as one may come to doubt her femininity because she has been conditioned to exhibit behavior patterns that society says are incompatible with womanhood. Thus, when she "acts like a man" she is regarded as abnormal and lacking in feminine qualities and, in turn, she comes to regard herself as being sexually inadequate. In other cases, some women who have not necessarily been conditioned to behave in a masculine way, may experience doubts as to their sexual identity because of society's response to their physical appearance. A Trenton, New Jersey, woman explains how this affected her:

> People used to kid me a lot about my size. . . . My uncle would say that God meant me to be a boy and

then changed His mind when it was too late. . . . It was comments like that made it obvious to me that I was different from other girls. In elementary school I was always the tallest one in class, taller than the boys and of course the kids made fun of me. . . . In the fifth grade I even played Abe Lincoln in a school play because I had the height for the part. I didn't want the part, but the teacher made me take it. I felt ridiculous on the stage with all those people watching me. . . . In high school I had trouble getting dates because boys didn't want to go out with a giant. . . . I never wore heels and I walked around with my shoulders hunched over so that I would seem smaller. . . . These are all little things, but when you're young they are very important. They made me feel as though I really wasn't feminine. I wasn't petite and cute the way girls are supposed to be.

. . . getting married helped me feel more womanly, but it was getting pregnant that really did it. For some reason I had thought that I wouldn't be able to have children, but soon after my husband and I stopped using contraception, I became pregnant. Although I wanted children very badly, I almost feared stopping the contraception because I was afraid that my doubts about my femaleness would be confirmed. On the other hand, I felt I had to have a child to prove to myself that I could do the most important thing a woman is capable of doing.

What this woman and others like her are doing is confusing the statement "I am a mother" with "I am a woman," and using pregnancy to erase their doubts about their sexual identity. Sometimes this works and sometimes it does not. If a woman's doubts about herself are deep enough, the birth of a child may not alleviate them. Under this condition a woman may opt for repeated pregnancies in the hope that by having many children she will have a quantity of evidence to prove her womanhood. The end result is that she has more children than she needs or wants and is still hung up on the same problem. It would have been better if she had worked out her problem before becoming a mother. Asking an infant to provide her with a sexual identity is placing a very heavy burden on very young shoulders.

"Having children will give me something to do in my old age."

There are two variations of this faulty motive for motherhood. The first, and probably the more prevalent, is the fact that some women have children to assure themselves of companionship and security during their old age. The threat of the eventual loss of a husband, of brothers and sisters, and close friends can create, even in fairly young women, the fear of social isolation during their senior years. In addition, they may face the possibility of financial insecurity during their old age. In an attempt to lessen the impact of these eventualities, a woman may desire children who will care for her both emotionally and financially when she is no longer able to care for herself. Dr. Mark Flapan, in his article dealing with the motivations for childbearing, offers this statement from a woman he interviewed.

I see myself in a terribly lonely state when I'm old. I'll say to myself, maybe you better take out some kind of insurance policy. Maybe it would be a good idea to have a child.*

Exploitation of the child in this case is delayed, because the woman is actually saying, "Because I brought my child into the world and cared for him when he was young, he must return the favor when I'm old." And this is a form of selfishness. Any adult, man or woman, who has a sense of personal responsibility should prepare for the time when his or her usual source of income dries up. People should not live carelessly and expect their children to pick up the tab later because their children just might not have the means to do so. Nor should parents expect their children to be their sole source of companionship during their senior years because this is a definite intrusion into their children's personal lives, an intrusion that no matter how much children love their parents, they may come to resent. This means that in addition to having financial self-sufficiency, women should develop social self-sufficiency.

The second variation of this motive for motherhood is having children in the hope of eventually having grandchildren. For a good part of their lives women feel needed and appreciated because of their role in caring for their homes and their children. However, a woman may look forward unhappily to the day when her children will grow up and leave her to set up homes of their own. At that point she may think that her usefulness will come to

* Flapan, p. 412.

an end. Not having been trained to look for alternatives to the job of being a mother, she may decide that when her own children are gone she will face a life of boredom. However, if she has grandchildren, and preferably lots of them, she will continue to be needed and she will continue to do the only thing she knows how to do, care for children. As a grandmother she will be called upon to baby-sit. And perhaps even more important, she will be able to reestablish through her grandchildren the love relationship she had with her own children. Certainly having many children increases the likelihood of having many grandchildren and a guarantee of plenty of jobs for Grandma to do, but Dr. Radkin views the situation differently:

> The only reason to have a child these days is to have grandchildren in order to retire. That's not the answer. Don't have children to have children to have grandchildren because you're exploiting children when you've got nothing to do. The question to solve is the retirement problem or the leisure-time problem. People don't know what to do with themselves when they have free time.

In other words, the women should solve the problem of free time themselves, and not through their children or grandchildren.

"Being a mother will give me something to do."
It is a simple fact of life that men, almost exclusively, hold the well-paying, interesting, and important jobs while women get the left-overs. Seldom do you find a

man working as a typist, a stenographer, or a file clerk because these jobs are low in pay, low in interest, and *very* low in status. And this of course makes them "women's work." In many cases, women who tire of this kind of work, and who see no alternative employment opportunities turn to motherhood in the hope that having children will fill their lives with purpose. Then again, there are wives whose male chauvinist husbands beat their chests and bellow, "No wife of mine is going to work!" and commit their wives to the house or apartment to stare at daytime TV. For these men, being the sole supporter of the household is an important masculinity trip, but for their wives it means an existence of isolation and dissatisfaction. So for many women, childbearing becomes a way to escape the boredom and loneliness their thoughtful husbands work hard to provide.

The problem with this motive for motherhood, aside from its exploitative aspect, is that the job of being a mother doesn't go on forever, actually it has a rather brief duration. A man can look forward to a good 40 or 45 years of useful and profitable employment, but a woman, in her role as mother, is really needed for only about 17 years per child, and of that time only the age span from infancy to early adolescence requires her full-time attention. During the teen-age years children become increasingly self-reliant if their mother has done a good job in raising them, and by 17 or 18 years of age they are off to college or beginning their careers. Then, at approximately 21 years of age, young men and women begin to think about starting their own families. So where does this leave Momma? If she hasn't developed any marketable skills she may find herself even more lonely and bored than she was before her first pregnancy.

For certain women, the inevitable maturation of their children creates fairly severe emotional difficulties. Dr. Henry Haberfeld talks about one of the most prevalent:

> Some women revel in the obligations they have toward their children. . . . Many women get depressed when their children grow up and grow away from them. One of the recognized causes of middle-age depression is the fact that women have outgrown their motherly role.

When asked if the development of commercial talents during the mothering years to be used when the children have grown up would help women avoid middle-age depression, Dr. Haberfeld replied, "One would like to think so. That is what I would recommend."

The increasing number of women with grown children returning to work and the definite trend to combine childbearing with a career clearly indicates that mothers are getting the message and realizing that bringing up children isn't the only outlet for their talents, interests, and abilities. However, a good number of wives, like this Stamford, Connecticut, mother of four, see motherhood as the only way to fill their lives with purpose and meaning:

> I love having small children around. They make the house come alive. . . . I had my second child soon after my oldest boy started school. With him away for a good part of the day there just wasn't that much to

do . . . you can only do so much cooking and washing. . . . I became pregnant with my daughter when my second son was in the first grade. . . . My youngest boy was born when my daughter was in second grade. . . . I'd like to have another baby, I'm still capable, but my husband doesn't want another child. He says four is enough. I guess he's right, but I still can't help thinking how quiet things will be with no children around.

In a later part of the interview this woman said that one of the reasons she wasn't thinking about going to work was because she had no idea of what she was capable of doing. It had been many years since she had held a job and she thought that her skills were either rusty or obsolete. This is a submotive for motherhood. Staying home with one child creates a psychological climate conducive to repeated pregnancies. A woman who has spent many years at home with her children may become fearful of returning to the business world because she doubts her ability to compete with adults in unfamiliar routines. She may believe that her lack of experience will place her in an unimportant job from which she would not derive the same attention, appreciation and fulfillment, found in her role as mother. A woman like this probably had her first child as a way of finding something to do and her subsequent children because she felt she had no other job options.

The following three faulty motives for motherhood deal more with a woman's desire for the physical state of pregnancy than with her wish for a baby. There are women who see the condition of being pregnant as an end in itself. For them, pregnancy holds certain symbolic psycho-social values which they hope will satisfy their particular pattern of emotional needs.

"Being pregnant will make me someone special."

There are women who go through childhood, adolescence, and young adulthood feeling that they have never received their fair share of affection or attention. A woman from a large family may have felt neglected because her mother's love and attention had to spread out over a number of children. Another woman may have had a sickly brother or sister who monopolized her parents' concern, or she may have had an exceptionally talented or intelligent sibling who was the focus of her mother's and father's attention. Then there is the possibility that an unattractive woman may have suffered because she had trouble attracting boys. For these and a multitude of other reasons, real or imagined, certain women look forward to becoming pregnant so that they will be able to demand and get the love, concern, and attention they believe has been denied them. In their article, "On the Need to Be Pregnant," Doctors Lerner, Raskin, and Davis write about this motive for pregnancy:

A woman may become pregnant primarily to gratify infantile needs for affection and attention. The pregnancy may give her a socially acceptable reason for an extreme self-love and she may become totally preoccupied with herself. This may approach a hypochondriacal state leading to repeated contacts with her physician whose reassurances she may then perceive as love.*

Almost everyone is familiar with the kind of woman who, when the doctor tells her she is pregnant, becomes a virtual invalid and expects everyone around her—husband, parents, and children—to do things for her that she is quite capable of doing herself. To talk to her you would think that no one besides herself has gone through a pregnancy and that no woman in history is suffering the way she is suffering. This of course is an obvious play to extract pity and attention from her family which she interprets as reassurances of their love. Some women will use their pregnancies as an excuse to let themselves go, to indulge themselves by overeating and oversleeping. "I'm eating for two," she will say, or "I must have my rest." And then there are the doctors, those wonderful, patient, and concerned saints whom they call daily for consoling words of advice. As Lerner, Raskin, and Davis point out, the contact that some pregnant women have with their physicians is a very important part of the pregnancy because it provides additional attention and a feeling that someone is always ready to take their small problems seriously. For such women, pregnancy is their finest hour and they go to all extremes to exploit their physical condition in order to make up for any previous years of neglect.

All this would not be so bad if pregnancy were not so

* Lerner, Raskin, and Davis, "On the Need to Be Pregnant," *International Journal of Psycho-Analysis*, (Vol. 48, 1967) p. 295.

fleeting. A woman can only live in the Pregnancy Paradise for nine months. Then she is faced with the stark realization that she is expected to care for a baby she really did not want and, worse yet, a baby who will probably receive a great deal of affection and attention from its father and grandparents; affection and attention the mother will feel is being taken from her. In the long run, the birth of a child cancels out the short-term benefits the woman enjoyed during her pregnancy. The child now is someone special and the mother has to give up her place of prominence. This may cause certain mothers to resent their babies which is obviously not a particularly auspicious beginning for the mother-child relationship.

Sometimes a woman who feels that her child is receiving too much attention may decide to become pregnant again in an attempt to regain the limelight. This cycle of futility may repeat itself several times before the woman realizes that she does not achieve permanent status merely by becoming pregnant.

Unmarried women who allow themselves to become pregnant in an effort to force their boyfriends to marry them are also using pregnancy as an affection-getting device. A woman who is unsure of her man's intentions sees pregnancy as a way to get him off the fence and down the aisle. But in many cases this doesn't work because the shock of learning that he is going to be a father may simply frighten him away.

Married women can have a very similar need for pregnancy. If a wife suspects, rightly or wrongly, that her husband is being unfaithful she may become pregnant in an effort to compete with the other woman. Because of her pregnancy a wife can expect her husband to be more attentive, take over some of the household responsibilities, and be less likely to cavort with his paramour. The difference between this motive for pregnancy and the "having a child will save my marriage" reason for motherhood is that the latter represents a long-term expectation that the marriage will remain intact, while the former is a stopgap measure, an immediate way of dealing with the threatened loss of a husband's affections. Like all the other faulty motives, it may or may not work. And if it doesn't, it is ultimately the child who will suffer the most.

"I got what I deserved."

In the first chapter we talked about the tendency of some people to regard parenthood as an atonement for committing the "sin" of sexual intercourse. They use the birth of a child as evidence, both to themselves and others, that they really weren't having a good time in bed but rather that they were respecting God's command to be fruitful and multiply. In many respects pregnancy serves the same purpose, especially for unmarried women who feel premarital coitus is a sin. Lerner *etal*, refer to this as the "guilt and pain dependence" motive.* This motive means that a woman uses her pregnancy as self-punishment for her sexual behavior. She feels that the pain, discomfort, and physical distortions of pregnancy will atone for her evil-doings. Or she may hope to become pregnant because she fears that her promiscuity will render her sterile. Becoming pregnant means that she has been forgiven and that everything is all right. Generally

* Lerner, Raskin, and Davis, p. 296.

these may be unconscious reasons for becoming pregnant, but nonetheless, they compel a surprising number of women to seek pregnancy. A caseworker with the New York City Department of Social Services remembers one such woman:

About two and a half or three years ago I had a client, a 19-year-old girl who applied for p.a. (public assistance) because she was seven months pregnant, unmarried, and had no one to support her. She had just quit her job because her pregnancy was obvious and she felt embarrassed since everyone knew she didn't have a husband. She told me that her parents weren't willing to help out because they were disgusted with her. . . . They were morally very straight and I guess they just disowned her when they learned she was going to have a baby. In fact, when she applied for welfare she was living in a girl friend's apartment because her father didn't want her in the house . . . but she really wasn't too disturbed about the whole thing. She made no effort to help us find the father and she wasn't angry with her parents. She seemed to feel that the pregnancy and later, her child, was her cross and she had to bear it. . . . Once I had a very long talk with her and she told me she felt terribly guilty for having sexual relations with a man she's only known for a brief time and that becoming pregnant was her punishment. . . . I mean she really believed that God was punishing her for enjoying sex. . . .

Most of us are conditioned to expect some kind of punishment if we break moral or legal rules and often when we are punished we feel better; we have paid for our wrongdoings and everything is squared away. "I have been punished" to too many individuals means "I have been forgiven," and the need for forgiveness is an ego need. Being forgiven gives us back our self-esteem, it means we are no longer bad or sinful. This girl welcomed her pregnancy although she knew she wasn't at all capable of caring for a child, because it meant both divine punishment and divine forgiveness, both of which were necessary to restore her feeling of personal worth. Of course she had no choice but to accept the pregnancy as abortions were illegal in New York at that time, but chances are that even if she had been able to get an abortion she wouldn't have. If a woman wants to engage in self-recrimination for her sexual behavior, that is her business. But what this woman and those like her are really doing is losing sight of the fact that eventually their children will also have to pay for their sins. When an unmarried woman becomes pregnant and says, "I got what I deserved," she should ask herself if her child will also be getting what it deserves.

"I enjoy the feeling of being pregnant."

Pregnancy means different things to different women. Ultimately of course, it means motherhood, but many mothers-to-be do not look that far ahead, and indeed for certain women the birth of a child may be the least desirable consequence of an otherwise ego-satisfying experience. Lerner, Raskin, and Davis provide an excellent discussion of this motive for pregnancy:

. . . there are women who prefer a pregnant body because of meanings they have attached to it which are peripheral or even antithetical to the realistic biological and social significance of pregnancy.

The swelling of the abdomen may represent an inner growth, a penis, that makes a pregnant woman feel complete "down below" and overcomes an existing sense of castration. She may get support and help from the idea that she has part of a man, of her husband, or father, inside her. The bodily changes occurring during pregnancy may alleviate a painful sense of emptiness, hollowness and numbness and serve as a defense against depersonalization. The swollen and full abdomen and the engorged breasts may decrease anxiety concerning bodily adequacy.*

There are many peripheral meanings to pregnancy, but for some women these can become primary. The Lerner, Raskin, and Davis article talks about the possibility of a woman wanting pregnancy to feel complete "down below" and makes reference to the idea that being pregnant may overcome a feeling of castration. According to Freudian theory, a young girl is believed to experience "penis envy" when she comes to realize that she does not have the large and imposing organ that a boy has. At this psychological moment, a girl wants to be a boy. However, this wish is later committed to the unconscious when she identifies with her mother and begins to accept her female role. Later in life, said Freud, this wish for a

* Lerner, Raskin, and Davis, pp. 295-296.

penis may express itself in the desire to become pregnant because the abdominal protrusion occurring during pregnancy represents a bodily extension symbolic of the longed-for penis. In addition, the possibility of having a male child means that a woman can actually create from her own body the valued organ she desired when she was young. There are many who accept this aspect of psychoanalytic theory, and those who actively reject it. We believe that girls may not envy boys their penises so much as their roles. In adult life, women learn that having a male child is more socially desirable than having a female child. Often the desire for pregnancy arises from a woman's desire to: 1. vicariously experience through her male child that which she missed as a girl; and 2. to have a boy child in the hope of winning social status.

Depersonalization, the feeling of a loss of identity, may provide a woman with a motive for pregnancy. The feelings and sensations of pregnancy, the pain and the visible aspects of the condition may make a woman think "I'm alive, I feel things. I have life inside me. I am a person. I am me." Descartes said, *Cogito, ergo sum*, I think, therefore I am. A pregnant woman may say, "I feel, therefore I am." Then too, pregnancy may represent a woman's attempt to assert her existence in a social sense, as we discussed under the heading, "Being pregnant will make me someone special."

The need for the condition and feelings of pregnancy is so important to some women that they experience *pseudocyesis*, spurious pregnancy. Their stomachs swell, their breasts become enlarged, they even may commence labor. Pseudocyesis clearly indicates emotional problems, but it does have one advantage over real pregnancies. No unwanted children are born simply because a woman wants to experience the feeling of being pregnant.

So far we have examined several highly personal reasons for desiring motherhood. Each of those motives sprang from an individual woman's ego needs. Thus they may be called psychogenic motives for motherhood, or motives created from within. There are also external forces that may encourage women to bear children. The force of these sociogenic motives was driven home by a female sociologist who summarized her speech on motherhood and women's liberation by saying:

Within our present social context, it is difficult, if not impossible for married women to remain childless. The socio-cultural pressures exerted by family, friends, and, in certain cases, religious tradition both overtly and covertly instill childbearing motives within the minds of women. No matter how strongly married women desire to postpone childbearing for an indefinite period of time, or, perhaps, avoid it altogether, the expectations and demands of the various social environments frequently force them to become mothers. It is indeed a rare and determined female who can remain childless beyond the first five to seven years of marriage in order to pursue a career or higher education . . . and before all women, not only those involved in women's liberation, can accept the idea—let's not call it an idea, let's call it a fact—that womankind is capable of selecting alternatives to motherhood it is imperative that the social constellation be rearranged in order to encompass, accommodate, and accept the realization that women can strive for goals other than motherhood and still be considered women. Until this happens women's liberation will face a long and slow uphill climb. A woman can't be liberated from the idea that motherhood is the only social door open to her until society is liberated from the faulty idea that women have only one natural role in the social structure.

There is no question that many women have children against their wishes or sooner than they had desired because they are unable to withstand the pressures from their parents, in-laws, friends, or church. The following three wrong reasons for motherhood reflect the need of certain women to win social acceptance. For these women a birth certificate is really a peace treaty with society; "There, I've had my baby. Now my family can stop nagging, my friends won't gossip and my way of life is in accordance with my religious beliefs." Are these also selfish and exploitative reasons for having children? Of course they are. Like the psychogenic motives they are attempts to satisfy some need or meet some expectation through the vehicle of motherhood.

"Having a child will please my parents."

What could be more altruistic than having a baby to please Mom and Dad? After all, they are getting along in years and need grandchildren to fill their empty hours. As one young mother put it, "My mother invested a lot in me. And the least I could do was to give her dividends on her investment. If grandchildren will make her happy, then I feel it's the least I can do for her after all she's done for me." That *sounds* fine, but this woman is using her children to prove to her own mother that she still is a good daughter, a daughter who does what mother wants. In addition, she is using her children as gifts to assure herself of her mother's continued appreciation. And finally, she is attempting to relieve herself of the burden of being indebted to her mother. No one says that a daughter, or a son for that matter, should not feel gratitude toward their parents, but it is questionable if giving grandchildren is the wisest way of showing that gratitude.

Then there was the woman who said, "Our family was always close, but when my sister had her first child, my husband and I saw much less of my parents because they liked to spend time with their grandchild. . . . I wouldn't say that was the only reason why we had a baby sooner than we expected, but it was a consideration." Shades of sibling rivalry! This woman sounds as though she had her baby so that she could compete more effectively with her sister. Unfortunately an older woman who plays favorites with her daughters may also do so with her grandchildren. And the woman who had her child to compete for her mother's attention may well find that her sister or brother has produced the favored grandchild.

Another factor encouraging a woman to have children in order to please her parents is guilt. A woman may feel that she has neglected her father and mother, that she has not been an attentive daughter, or that she has thought too little about her parents' happiness. Often these feelings of guilt are exacerbated by some family tragedy. A former fashion and TV model explains why she gave up her career for motherhood:

> You couldn't say that I was close with my mother, even though I was an only child. . . . I went out of town to college when I was 17 and I usually found summer jobs as dramatic counselor at sleep-away camps or at resort hotels where women brought their children. . . . I had majored in dramatics, but you can starve before you get work so I did some modeling to make money. Soon I gave up on acting and concentrated only on modeling. It paid very well, it was interesting and I guess I hoped that someone would see me in a commercial and want me for an acting part. . . . I married about two years after college. . . . About two years after that Dad got sick. . . . When he died, Mother started calling me more often. She was lonely, her old friends still had their husbands and she felt out of place. . . . I began to feel sorry for her. I thought about how distant we had been and how I should be able to do something for her now that she didn't have anyone. . . . She began talking about grandchildren and about how they would mean so much to her. . . . I wasn't really ready to give up modeling, things were going very well, and there was some hope of a part in a TV daytime drama. . . . I felt that I was somehow responsible for her loneliness. . . . I had never given her much pleasure, in fact she was very much against my acting plans and my modeling. She didn't think they were "worthwhile" careers. . . . When I did become pregnant, mother almost moved in. There

wasn't enough she could do for me. And when the baby was born she was in seventh heaven. . . . Frankly, I still haven't gotten used to the idea of being home so much. I'm really not happy being a housewife and I do miss my work. . . . But I don't know which is the lesser of the two evils. Feeling miserable because I'm stuck in the house, or feeling guilty because my mother is alone and I'm the only one—that is, the baby and me, who can provide her with some sort of company. . . . She has offered to take care of the baby while I work, but I didn't go for that. It would probably mean that she'd have to move in and neither my husband nor I want her to. . . .

The need to be a good daughter, the attempt to win parental affection and attention, or the desire to ease the guilt of years of parental neglect all offer motives for motherhood, but they are faulty motives. Once again the mother is assigning her children a task they must perform to insure her love. If they fail she may behave in a negating manner and nothing in the world is more pitiable than an unwanted child, even if he was once tied with pink or blue ribbons and offered as a gift of love to Grandma or Grandpa.

"Without children you're an outsider."
There are two social imperatives that women have to obey if they expect to keep their friends and maintain a "normal" social life. The first is that they must marry. There is no one lonelier than a single woman whose girl friends all have husbands. The second is that after mar-

riage they must have children. Married women without children soon find they have little in common with their friends who have become mothers. Expectant mothers will get together and talk about their pregnancies, their doctors, and plans for their children. The unpregnant woman cannot participate in these conversations and she senses an encroaching isolation that will increase after her friends give birth. Once women have their babies, their whole pattern of life changes. They have different interests, greater limitations on their freedom, more responsibilities, and an entirely new set of activities that are essentially child-centered.

The childless woman really does not fit in, leaving her two alternatives: 1. find new friends who do not have children; and 2. become pregnant and join the club. Although the first may be more practical, the second often appears easier. In many cases the woman was planning to have children anyway but had intended to wait in order to accumulate money by working, to help her husband complete school, or to complete her own education. The social pressure of being the only one among her friends without children merely induces her to have children sooner than she had expected:

> Harold and I never thought about not having children, said a young housewife and mother, but we did want to wait a few years. Hal was teaching high school and he was taking his M.A. at night. I was teaching in an elementary school. . . . We wanted to save up enough money so that we could live comfortably until I was able to go back to work. . . . We were also planning to

go to Europe for an entire summer and we were putting aside money for that. . . . It wasn't only the fact that all our friends either had children or were expecting children that made us change our minds about waiting, but I have to admit it did influence our thinking. When you're surrounded by babies you start thinking babies and gradually other things become less important. The trip for instance. . . . With the money we were planning on using for our vacation we had enough to meet expenses and enough left over for emergencies. . . . I remember that before the baby was born I didn't have too much in common with my friends. Without children you're an outsider, you find it hard to come up with things to talk about when you get together with your girl friends. The conversation always turns to children and if you don't have children, you're left out. . . . It's almost as though they're in a different world, girls I've known almost all my life suddenly become different, strangers, when they become mothers. . . .

Social isolation from friends who have become mothers is one motive for childbearing, but this is an indirect form of social pressure. There is a similar motive that results from a more direct application of social pressure. A suburban woman says:

We bought our house not because we wanted our future children to grow up away from the city, but because we couldn't take Manhattan anymore. Just because we worked in the crowds, and the noise and filth didn't mean we had to live with them. . . . Sure, the commuting takes time, but it's worth it. . . . I didn't realize though that our lives would be so carefully watched by neighbors. Living in the city all our lives we've grown accustomed to people minding their own business. But out here if you sneeze, the neighbors from blocks away come in to say *gesundheit*. . . . All the women out here have kids and if you don't have kids you've really got no one to talk to. . . . They're always somewhere . . . doing something with their kids. . . . That's what started me thinking about having children. I always knew I'd have to have children sometime. Being a woman it's expected of you and I guess I wanted them. . . . The thing though that really made me decide not to wait any longer were the questions that centered around my not having children. "When are you and Marty having children?" "Isn't that why you moved here? I mean for the children's sake . . . ?" And then I heard that someone was saying I wasn't having children because either my husband or I had something wrong with us. I found that out when a neighbor told me a story about a friend of hers who had adopted a child and "no one ever knew." When I asked her why she was telling me this she told me about the rumor. . . . I figured that as long as it was inevitable, I might as well have a baby now. . . .

It is interesting to note that this woman never questioned the idea that having children was the only alternative open to a normal woman. If she had not been indoctrinated with this ridiculous notion there is a good chance that she would have been able to resist the influences of her neighbors' natalistic pressure.

"My religion expects married women to have children."

Certain religious faiths, notably the Roman Catholic and the Orthodox Jewish, are quite clear in their demands that women should bear children, although for slightly different reasons. As Betty Rollin pointed out in her *Look Magazine* article, the Roman Catholic dogma concerning sexuality and procreation is based on the Augustinian proclamation that intercourse between a married couple is sinful if there is no intention of bearing children. That means that a woman can either remain chaste after marriage or take her chances with the rhythm system which almost invariably means having children. In the Orthodox Jewish tradition, childbearing is considered a woman's main function with the ultimate goal of having male children. There is a great premium placed on a woman's ability to have sons, so much so in fact that if the first born is a boy the child is considered an offering from God Himself. When this happens there is a ceremony called a *pid-yon-a-ben* which involves a symbolic purchase of the child from God. The birth of a girl goes somewhat unheralded. In both the Jewish and the Catholic religions motherhood is expected and women who wish to adhere to these faiths must bear children. Of course everyone is entitled to their particular religious beliefs, but sometimes, especially in the case of childbearing, those beliefs are too rigid and impersonal. A mother involved in a Bronx welfare rights organization declares:

> My husband is a Catholic but he isn't religious. . . . When we got married he told me I had to use the pill because we couldn't afford to have no children. He didn't want me to stop working because we had lots of bills to pay. . . . For a while I took the pill but I felt like I was doing something wrong, like I was commiting a sin or something. . . . I talked to the priest and told him we didn't have no money and that my husband didn't want kids. He told me that using the pill was going against the Church and the Pope. He said that we could only use the rhythm system. I told my husband what the priest said and my husband said that he didn't care, he still didn't want me to stop using the pill. But I stopped anyway. I didn't tell him. . . . I tried to be careful but I got pregnant anyway and my husband got angry. He even wanted me to have an abortion but I said no. . . . When I had to quit my job my husband couldn't pay all the bills and they took away some of our furniture. . . . We went to the welfare department but we couldn't get any money because my husband was earning too much. . . . After the baby was born my husband lost his job. He was drinking and he was late and many times he didn't go to work. . . . He got unemployment but he left one day. No one knows where he went. . . . Then I got welfare. . . . I don't like living on welfare and I want the city to give day care clinics so that women like me can go to work and earn our own money. . . .

When asked if she had changed her mind about her religion, this woman replied:

> You mean am I still a Catholic? I was born Catholic and I'm going to die a Catholic. . . . The Church may be a little old-fashioned, but the Pope will change the rule about birth control when he sees how much problems it causes for the poor people. You wait. You'll see. The Church won't forget the poor people.

Many surveys indicate that increasing numbers of women of all faiths are using birth control methods, even if it means going against their religious beliefs. However, there are still many whose consciences and sense of morality would suffer greatly if they did use contraception. For them the choice is difficult, procreation or abstinence, and that is really no choice at all. Can religious motives for childbearing be considered wrong motives?

In reviewing the wrong reasons for motherhood we must remember that they often reinforce each other. For example, a woman may decide to have children because she wants to prove her femininity, derive status through childbearing, and provide her own parents with grandchildren. This is not to say that there might not be one motive that is more important than the others, but most women express a variety of needs when they become mothers.

In the ideal situation, mothers would only have children to provide the world with self-reliant, anxiety-free, non-hostile, and non-resentful youngsters who will grow up to be responsible, self-confident, and compassionate adults. This can only happen if children are reared in an environment in which they are accepted for themselves and loved for who they are and not for what they can do. Children who grow up fearing that one wrong step can plunge them into maternal disfavor are children who were conceived in selfishness. Any woman who has a child with the intention of using that child to overcome personal, marital, or social problems has no business becoming a mother.

III

The Wrong Reasons
for Fatherhood

Although women are more physically, psychologically, and socially involved in parenthood, men also experience powerful and compelling motives that make parenthood desirable and necessary. And like women, many of their motives are egotistical and faulty. In many cases the difference between the wrong motives for motherhood and the wrong motives for fatherhood is more a difference in degree than in kind. Because men have a greater variety of alternatives open to them, they tend to be less preoccupied with parenthood.

Nonetheless, men *do* want to have children and they want them, in certain respects, for the same reasons as their wives. A young husband unsure of his "grown-upness" may use fatherhood as a way of showing that he is a mature and responsible family man. Some men, like some women, may have the curious idea that they have to pay for their pleasures and want to become fathers to avoid guilt feelings arising from their sexual behavior. Or a man who feels that he does not stand much of a chance of making anything out of his life may look forward to having a son who will make good. And of course religious tradition can be just as important to a man as it is to a woman.

Probably most, or perhaps all, of the wrong reasons for motherhood can be equally applied to men. Selfish reasons for having children are not sexually heteronomous. However, it is possible to isolate some faulty reasons that seem to be more common to men, and these result from the differences in the socialization process and not from innate differences in biology.

From boyhood, males are taught that becoming a man means being dominant, competitive, aggressive, protective of women, and virile. In striving to live up to these ideals, men may develop hang-ups which they think can be resolved by the birth of a child. From these hang-ups sprout the five masculine emotional and social situations that encourage fatherhood for the wrong reasons.

Macho

The Spanish word for manhood, *macho*, summarizes in its two syllables the entire complex of ideas and assumptions that we have concerning the behavior of "real men." *Macho* means strength and bravery. *Macho* means both physical and psychological dominance over women. And *macho* means virility.

During middle childhood a boy starts thinking of what he will be when he grows up. Usually his ideas center around jobs that require strength and bravery and offer excitement. The popular "fireman-policeman-cowboy-astronaut" response indicates that most boys associate manhood with these qualities. Later, during the adolescent years, they become concerned with souped-up cars and motorcycles. Aside from the fact that cars and bikes symbolize freedom and independence from parents, they also signify sexual identity. When a teen-ager guns his engine, the loud roar is an attempt at masculine self-assertion. And when he takes foolish chances on the road he is trying to show how brave he is.

As teen-agers, boys also want to prove their masculinity by obviously dominating their girl friends. They tend to equate maleness with callous indifference. Later, as husbands, their views soften to the more traditional concept that a woman *needs* a man to protect her, provide her with the essentials of life, and offer her security. In return, she is expected to be submissive and yielding. And despite the new movement toward women's liberation, society generally labels those girls who don't exhibit these "feminine" qualities as castrating.

Along with the notion of male dominance comes the idea that virility and manhood are one and the same. Any adolescent boy who wants to establish his masculinity tells his friends how many "chicks he scored with." And the belief that only a quantity of seductions indicate a man's *macho* frequently outlasts adolescence. Grown men will get together and talk about all the girls they "had" in their youth and of all the women they are now fooling around with on the side. In certain instances, probably more than we know, this kind of conversation is an unconscious attempt to combat the anxiety created by fears of possible latent homosexual tendencies. Every time a man boasts about his sexual activities, he may be trying to convince himself and his friends that he is 100 percent male without one iota of "faggot" in him.

For men who have to advertise their sexual exploits in order to affirm their masculinity, marriage can create problems. It is not acceptable for a husband to tell his friends about his intimacies with his wife which means that he has no way of letting people know about his sexual prowess, unless he becomes a father. Obviously if a man's wife has children, he has been making love to her and if she has lots of children he has really been keeping her busy. In fact, there are far too many men who have more children than they need or can afford because a quantity of sons and daughters provides visual evidence of their ability to perform in bed. A case worker with the New York City Department of Social Services tells about an extreme case of this type:

On my caseload I've got a family receiving Home Relief. . . . The husband works as the super of an apartment house but he doesn't make nearly enough money to support his wife and family . . . he's got ten kids. . . . When I first got this case he had nine children. . . . Soon after he came to tell me that his wife was pregnant again. . . . I can't remember his exact words, but he was obviously proud of the fact that his wife was expecting again and he said something to the effect of, "I'm 56 and still going . . ." He couldn't care less that every child he had was an added burden on the taxpayers. He felt, and he told me as much, that it was his right to have as many children as he wanted. . . . When the tenth child was born he stenciled a big sign that said, "Number 10. It's a boy. . . ." I'd be willing to bet that he has at least one more child, maybe more. . . . The person I feel sorry for is his wife. . . .

The sign this man placed in his window may have been an expression of fatherly pride and happiness at the birth of another child. But it also could have been this man's way of telling the neighborhood that he was a real man because he had managed to impregnate his wife for a tenth time, even at the ripe old age of 56.

A good part of the *macho* motive for fatherhood rests on the idea that sex implies conquest of the female and that conquering a woman, even your wife, is a very manly thing to do. When a man tries to seduce a woman and she refuses he often interprets this as an act of castration. Such men also assume that it must be the man who does the seducing. Many men resent "forward" women because their sexually aggressive behavior does not allow these men to exercise their *macho*. For many men the idea of forcing themselves on unwilling women intensifies the erotic enjoyment of intercourse. This becomes evident when we hear husbands saying, "I don't let my wife get away with any of that 'I don't feel like it tonight' crap. She knows she'd better be ready when I'm ready or tough." So when a man has many children he is also saying that he has intercourse when he pleases and as many times as he pleases. However, the younger generation is probably not pressured by this motive for fatherhood. Psychiatrist Richard Radkin explains why:

With the Sexual Revolution you won't get a guy who is upset whether he's a man or not. . . . You're talking about a guy who has to have four kids to prove he can fuck. And they don't bother doing that anymore than they tell you what they had for dinner to prove that they can eat.

If what the doctor says is correct it will mean that in the future unwanted children will not be conceived simply so their fathers can prove to the world, "I am a man!"

For the present, however, virility and masculinity are still closely associated. In Manchester, England, Alan Jones, a research chemist at the University of Manchester, received a $180,000 grant to develop a male anti-fertility drug. Upon receiving the grant, Mr. Jones explained that such research had to be done at a university because the commercial drug companies were nervous about tampering with the male reproductive system. We all know that except for the condom, the major birth control devices currently available, including the pill and the diaphragm, are used by *women*. Does this mean that the men who direct the drug industry have unconscious reservations about interfering with male fertility? Or, have they done market research and found that it would be unprofitable to manufacture these drugs because men, fearing that their *macho* would suffer, will refuse to take birth control pills? Possibly the answer involves a little bit of each.

King Kong

The film *King Kong* contains the line: "The natives call him Kong, but we'll call him King Kong because he is master of all he surveys." How many men would like to be the undisputed rulers of their domains? Obviously a majority. Society instills them with a need for dominance, but often does not provide the means of fulfilling that need. The truth is, most men are not their own boss. What we really have is a nation of vassals who are conditioned to think of themselves as rulers and suffer anxiety because their lives are dominated by so many forces outside their control. The one major area of dominance that society does provide the average man with is fatherhood. When a man becomes a father he can demand respect and obedience from his children. As the head of a household he has power, not only over his wife, but over several other human beings as well. And some men have large families because it increases the "territory" over which they can reign, thereby offering extra support to their weak egos.

The power motive for fatherhood is definitely exploitative. Men who feel they cannot measure up to the social expectations of manhood use their children as a barrier against feelings of emasculation. Said a salesclerk and father of four, "All day I have to take crap from customers and supervisors. But when I get home at night, things are done *my* way." This man, and millions like him, are the victims of the ridiculous idea that men are inherently aggressive and dominant and that a failure to exhibit these traits undercuts their manhood. Nothing can be further from the truth. The fact of the matter is that conditioning, not genetics, is responsible for the dominance of males and the submissiveness of females. And that means that a man can be something less than the supreme ruler of his home and still biologically maintain his manhood. This further means that once men can get it into their heads that they do not have to boss their wives and families around to assert their masculinity, then fewer children will be born to fill King Kong's needs for subjects.

Monopoly

Nothing could be more devastating to the frail egos of certain men than witnessing a full-scale invasion of the so-called "man's world" by an army of liberated females. This world encompasses both the business and professional communities as well as the fun side of the sexual double standard. Most husbands view any increase in female independence as a direct threat to their accustomed superiority. In an effort to maintain exclusive control, men have established a monopoly which, until recently, meant open and active job discrimination against females backed up by the almost foolproof tactic of impregnation which assured husbands that their wives would be home taking care of children and not out in the world competing and fraternizing with men. A recent poll taken by the American Association of University Women shows that the majority of American men still believe a woman's place is in the home. According to the results of this survey, 60 percent of the men questioned believe that a woman's major role is that of wife and mother. Most of the men surveyed were husbands which means there are two possible reasons for this finding. A great number of married men feel that if their wives are capable of holding well-paying jobs then their role as family provider would become less important. Even more threatening though is the possibility that their wives might actually earn more than they do. Consequently these men may use parenthood to handicap their wives in the financial arena.

The second reason why husbands might not want their wives to work is the fear that they might be tempted to enjoy extramarital relations. Men have conveniently established a double standard in this regard. It is all right for a man to quietly engage in affairs with other women because a man "needs variety." However, a woman who does the same thing is considered a tramp. And a wife who fools around with other men is really saying that her husband is not able to keep her satisfied, that he is not a real man. To protect themselves from this embarrassment, there are husbands who see having children as the best way of keeping their wives safely home. Some men even go so far as forbidding their wives to use birth control devices for fear of increasing the possibility of their wives being unfaithful. *Planned Parenthood*'s Ira Neiger discusses this situation:

> There are men who, for whatever reasons, don't like the idea of their wives using contraception. Some men think, for example, that if their wives are on the pill that they're apt to be more promiscuous because they're protected from pregnancy. This represents suspicion or even paranoia in some men.

And psychiatrist Dr. Robert E. Gould, in his excellent *New York Times Magazine* article, "The Wrong Reasons for Having Children," summarizes this outdated motive:

The Case Against Having Children

This kind of husband seldom faces the fact that his own insecurities are the basis of his "old-fashioned" philosophy. He fears that his wife may find the outside world of work (and other men) too desirable.*

Prosperity

During the first two or three years of marriage the chances are that a young couple will find it economically unfeasible to have children. It is very likely that during this time a wife will work until her husband completes his education, establishes himself in a business or profession, or receives a raise or promotion that will allow both of them to live on his income. Then, when the husband feels secure in his ability to provide adequately for a wife and family, his wife will quit her job and bear children. Unfortunately this very familiar pattern frequently encourages men toward fatherhood for the wrong reasons. A man who is financially secure may seek fatherhood simply because society expects it of him.

Perhaps an even more psychologically cogent motive for a man to become a parent than the desire to conform is the need he may have to prove to himself, his friends, and relatives that he is financially able to take on the costs of fatherhood. Just as men learn to equate their maleness with dominance and virility they also learn that masculinity has a dollar value. A husband who makes a good living, who does not have to rely on his wife's income is respected in the community as an excellent provider, and a wonderful husband.

* Robert E. Gould, "The Wrong Reasons for Having Children," *New York Times Magazine*, (May 3, 1970) p. 86.

92

The Wrong Reasons for Fatherhood

Men who have children as a way of showing their financial success tend to measure their personal worth by the size of their bank accounts. In many cases money substitutes for the qualities of manhood they feel may be lacking in their psychological makeup. And it is further very likely that these men actually have no interest in assuming the real responsibilities of fatherhood because that would interfere with their moneymaking activities. There are any number of executive and professional fathers who spend practically no time at all with their sons and daughters. Their only contact is with the bills they receive for the children's dental work, music lessons, and private schools. As they write the checks they feel they are being good fathers because they are giving their children the "best that money can buy." But this is often not good enough. Many delinquent or neurotic children come from "good homes," simply because their fathers took no meaningful interest in their upbringing.

Why do some men insist on having children? The answer is simple. Having children is an ego trip for them. Every time they goodnaturedly complain about the unbelievable amount it costs to "bring children up right" they are actually telling people how much money they have and that makes them feel like big men.

The Family Name

For some reason men seem to have a strong need to achieve immortality. This is not to say that many women do not look forward to a life after death, but this represents a spiritual desire whereas men often want to leave behind some physical or tangible evidence of their existence.

Great generals and kings erected monuments to themselves and ancient emperors, convinced that they were gods incarnate, had their images carved in stone in an attempt to impress future generations with their grandeur and power. The futility of such efforts has never been expressed better than in Percy Bysshe Shelley's great poem, *Ozymandias*:

> I met a traveller from an antique land
> Who said: Two vast and trunkless legs of stone
> Stand in the desert. . . . Near them, on the sand,
> Half sunk, a shattered visage lies, whose frown,
> And wrinkled lip, and sneer of cold command,
> Tell that its sculptor well knew those passions read
> Which yet survive, stamped on these lifeless things,
> The hand that mocked them, and the heart that fed:
> And on the pedestal these words appear:
> "My name is Ozymandias, king of kings:
> Look on my works, ye Mighty, and despair!"
> Nothing beside remains. Round the decay
> Of that colossal wreck, boundless and bare
> The lone and level sands stretch far away.

The average man, unlike Ozymandias, has neither the power nor the finances to construct a great statue of himself, but, like this ancient king, he does wish a sense of personal significance in the face of a forgetful eternity. Fatherhood often offers a way of fulfilling this need. If a man can have a child, or, more accurately, a son to whom he can pass on the family name, he feels he has achieved a degree of immortality. Such a man is actually using his child as a monument to himself. If there is a Thomas Thompson, Jr., listed in the telephone book in years to come then people must assume that a Thomas Thompson, Sr., once existed. Somewhat less poetically than Shelley but nonetheless as poignantly, Dr. Robert Gould explains why having a child in an effort to attain immortality is not a good motive for parenthood:

> . . . the baby provides a means to gratify vanity and an excuse for not achieving much else. A constructive, useful life, good work and good relationships are other ways to leave a mark on the world. A baby is not a substitute for any of these.*

These inadequate and faulty reasons for fatherhood, like the poor reasons for motherhood, are based on the expectation that children will help their fathers overcome certain psychological and social problems. Men who have children as a way of proving their manhood may find that the birth of a child, or even of many children does not make them any more of a man than they were before they become fathers. And men who want to achieve immortality through their sons are often forced to realize that the mere impregnation of their wives does not necessarily add great meaning to their lives. The resulting disappointment often makes a man hostile or apathetic toward his children because they did not live up to his selfish expectations. The best time for a man to work out his ego and sexual identity problems is before he becomes a father. In so doing he may find that he does not actually wish to become a parent. Or, as a result of having a better idea of who and what he is, he may just be a better father.

* Robert E. Gould, p. 85.

95

IV

The Case Against
Large Families

There are various "isms" that we fear will eventually bring about the downfall of our nation if they are left unchecked. We talk of the dangers of communism and fascism and we abhor the excesses of radicalism on our campuses. Yet there is one "ism" we cherish that is more dangerous in its far-reaching implications than all the others. This is the doctrine of natalism, the belief that individual couples have the right to have as many children as they please despite the scientific conviction that unchecked population expansion is by far the most potentially disastrous problem facing mankind in the middle of the twentieth century.

Natalism is to childbearing what *laissez-faire* is to capitalism. Under a *laissez-faire* economic system individual businessmen and corporations can expect no government interference in the running of business. The private sector of the economy has the absolute and unquestioned right to fix prices, pay labor what it wishes, create monopolies, corner resources, and drive competitors out of business with unfair practices. In short, a *laissez-faire* philosophy gives business a free hand to do as it pleases regardless of the public welfare. However, the economic history of the United States is in many ways a history of the development and enforcement of various regulations to limit the prerogatives of business and industry and to bring them into line with the public's best interests. The various anti-trust laws, interstate commerce regulations, and the establishment of minimum wage guidelines were instituted to guard society against the excesses, greed, and selfishness of individual entrepreneurs. But we have done little to protect society against the excesses, greed, and selfishness of people who insist on having large families that use up more than their fair share of available resources, contribute more than their fair share of pollution, and who receive tax allowances even though they require more than their fair share of government services.

Under our natalistic philosophy we protect the prerogative of couples to reproduce without restriction or condemnation. And we go one step further, we sanctify such behavior. Natalists point to the Bible and say that God Himself has given them the right and the moral duty to be "fruitful and multiply." However, they neglect to mention the obligations and responsibilities that God gave mankind along with the right to have children. In a more complete form, this quote from the Bible reads:

And God blessed them; and God said unto them: "Be fruitful, and multiply, and replenish the earth, and sub-

97

due it; and have dominion over the fish of the sea, and over the fowl of the air, and over every living thing that creepeth upon the earth."

The word "replenish" should not be limited to human beings, but should be understood in the broader sense. Man has the obligation to give back to the earth what he takes away from it. The ancient Hebrew practice of allowing farmland to lie fallow for a season after several seasons of cultivation is based on the biblical idea that periods of disuse give the earth back the fertility that farming takes from it. In this way man replenishes the earth. Large and growing populations work counter to this biblical directive. Vast numbers of people, created in a large measure by oversized families, use up resources faster than science can find substitutes for them and faster than nature can replace them. In many respects people who have large families are not accepting God's directive to replenish the earth because they expect a new god, Almighty Technology, to supply themselves and their families. Joel Hedgpeth, chief of the Yaquina Marine Biological Laboratory at Oregon State University, offers the following warning:

Those ecologists and engineers who seem to think that we can solve all our problems by manipulating our natural system to support an ever-increasing population are simply borrowing time that does not exist. Of course, if we want to live like ants under plastic domes to protect us from air pollution while eating some sort of sludge from artificially eutrophic ponds sustained by our own effluvia, we may last a bit longer as a species, at least as a species of ant.*

God, in His wisdom, gave mankind dominion over living things because He assumed that man with his intelligence would protect these fellow creations of God. However, He also gave man free will, free will to overpopulate the earth and to dump the by-products of his civilization into the waters to kill fish, and to pollute the air so that it is fit neither for man nor fowl, and to destroy the forests and fields, thereby wiping out entire species of animals that God Himself created. To those natalists who say that the right to have large families is a God-given right, it should be pointed out that God giveth and God taketh away and in the not-too-distant future man may find his right to reproduce taken away because overpopulation has made life on earth impossible.

In its most important aspect, the case against having children is a brief against large families which may be examined on two levels. On one level, large families create problems that reach beyond a particular home to the nation and to the world community. Almost all of the things that people claim to despise—poverty, disease, war, crime, and famine—have their roots in overpopulation. On another level, large families create emotional, financial, physical, and educational problems for individual children and their parents. On the whole, the world, our nation and the institution of the family can survive only if people limit their number of children.

* Joel W. Hedgepath, *Environment*, (Vol. 12 No. 3) p. 46.

The Case Against Having Children

Before we consider the broad social problem of over-population, it would be a good idea to define exactly what we mean when we say "a large family." In the past family size was determined by two factors, economics and child mortality. A family had to have sufficient children to help out with certain necessary chores and to compensate for the fact that an inevitable number could be expected to die during early childhood. Today, at least in the industrialized nations, those factors no longer exist. For most middle-class families children pose more of an economic burden than an economic benefit. It has been estimated that the average income family must spend between 25,000 to 30,000 dollars per child to raise that child correctly. And that *excludes* the costs of a college education! And the advances of modern medicine have substantially reduced the threat of fatal childhood diseases. Large families reflected certain needs of times gone by and many experts now consider any family having more than two children as large. The reason for this is as follows:

If we are to arrest the growth of U.S. population by the end of the century, the two-child family must voluntarily become the norm. Today an average of just under 2.2 children per-completed-family is required for replacement, but if the socially accepted norm were two children, the number of families which exceeded two would probably be more than those which had less than two, and the result might come close to replacement.*

* *Population Bulletin,* vol. XXVI, No. 1, April 1970, pp. 24-25.

The only exception that we would take to this line of reasoning is the assumption that married couples should replace themselves on a one-to-one basis, and that is not necessarily a good idea. In the first place not everyone needs to be or should become a parent, and in the second place one-to-one replacement means that we would stabilize the American population at its present 200 million. Dr. Paul R. Ehrlich, Professor of Biology at Stanford University, author of *The Population Bomb*, and President of Zero Population Growth, an organization working for population stabilization, believes that 150 million people would be the optimum population for the United States. At our present size we are faced with overburdening problems of housing in our urban areas, overcrowded schools, unemployment, and environmental deterioration. A decrease of 50 million people would make these problems easier and less expensive to solve.

But let us assume that one-to-one replacement *is* the correct target for the United States. The question then becomes, "What will happen if we do not achieve worldwide population stabilization before the end of the century?" To this the only answer is a gross magnification of the international problems we are already facing. We can expect the predictions that Thomas Malthus made 170 years ago to come true. His thesis is that disease, war, and famine of epidemic proportions will result when population outstrips the means of subsistence. We need not look back to nineteenth century predictions. Many living people are equally alarmed. Representative Morris K. Udall of Arizona paints a grim picture of the world if we continue to breed without reason:

The Case Against Having Children

If an ultimate calamity were to befall mankind—and in nuclear weapons we have the tools—chances are it will be population, not politics, that will have to be blamed. It does not take much imagination to see that the foundation of war can be laid in the mud of prospective Asian famine. The specter that Latin America's hundreds of millions will double *within the next generation* cannot spell anything but turbulence and misery —the very atmosphere that invites the spread of Castroism.

Yet, while the United States spends billions in an attempt to grapple with individual problems, we are still doing little to get to the basic problem! *The world's population cannot continue to grow at its present rate.* The earth cannot support unlimited numbers of people. If birth rates do not fall, death rates will rise.*

Representative Udall makes it clear that the United States must become a leader in the battle against world overpopulation. Judy Senderowitz, president of the New York City chapter of Zero Population Growth, agrees that America must not only be a leader in this struggle but that it must first attack its own population problems as a way of providing an example:

. . . The U.S. is important, number one, because the U.S. is a world leader and it does have to show that it's keeping its own house in order before it can say to other countries that they may possibly be in worse

* Morris K. Udall, "Standing Room Only on Spaceship Earth," *Arizona Magazine* (July 27, 1969).

shape, "You must limit your population." The second thing is that we have the technical capabilities and the educational capabilities to be able to spread the word and to carry out our own plans for the dissemination of birth control information. Thirdly, if we consider the amount of stress that the average American puts on the environment compared with the average citizen of India we would have a comparable population of four billion.

What Miss Senderowitz is referring to is Wayne Davis's idea of "Indian equivalents" which compares the negative effect that an American has on the land with that of an Indian. Professor Davis explains the basis for this comparison:

The average Indian eats his daily few cups of rice (or perhaps wheat, whose production on American farms contributed to our one percent per year drain in quality of our active farm land), draws his bucket of water from the communal well and sleeps in a mud hut. In his daily rounds to gather cow dung to burn to cook his rice and warm his feet, his foot steps . . . bring about a slow deterioration of the ability of the land to support people. His contribution to the destruction of the land is minimal.

An American, on the other hand, can be expected to destroy a piece of land on which he builds a home, garage and driveway. He will contribute his share to the 142 million tons of smoke and fumes, seven million junked cars, 20 million tons of paper, 48 billion cans, and 26 billion bottles the overburdened environment must absorb each year. To run his air conditioner we will strip-mine a Kentucky hillside, push the dirt and slate down into a stream, and burn coal in a power generator, whose smokestack contributes to a plume of smoke massive enough to cause cloud seeding and premature precipitation from Gulf winds which should be irrigating the wheat farms of Minnesota.

Thus I want to introduce a new term, which I suggest be used in further discussions of human population and ecology. We should speak of "Indian equivalents." An Indian equivalent I define as the average number of Indian citizens required to have the same detrimental effect on the land's ability to support human life as would the average American.

In Indian equivalents . . . the population of the United States is at least four billion.*

Unfortunately many Americans are not moved by this line of reasoning. The problem, as they see it, is not to limit the population growth of the United States but to assist India and other underdeveloped countries to achieve the same standard of living that we have. This however, cannot happen. The United States with its current population of approximately 200 million uses up about 55 percent of the world's available resources, leaving 45 percent for the other 3.3 billion people on our planet. Obviously then, it will not be possible for most other nations to achieve anything approaching our living standard if we continue to demand and consume the lion's share of the

* Wayne H. Davis, "Overpopulated America," *The New Republic*, January 10, 1970, pp. 13-14.

world's resources. The only way we can bring about some sort of equality in the distribution of needed resources is not necessarily by lowering our own standard of living but by stabilizing, or even better, by reducing our own population. American children consume many more times the goods and services that children in underdeveloped countries do. In fact five children overseas who would normally grow up in poverty and hunger can have the essentials of food and clothing and the "luxury" of a decent education for what it costs to raise one American child. If these things are unavailable to them because we insist on pursuing a policy of unrestricted natalism we had better hang on to those cans, bottles, and other by-products of our affluent civilization that Professor Davis talks about and use them to pile around our borders as a wall against the hungry and destitute multitudes whose resources we have selfishly used to maintain our unnecessarily large families.

But that wall will only protect us from without. What about the dangerous conditions created by overpopulation *within* our nation. If we do not put a halt to natalism the United States of America will have about 400 million people by the turn of the century and every upward movement of the population graph will bring us closer to self-destruction. And it is beginning to happen at this very moment. There are approximately 15 million hardcore hungry people in our country whose inability to afford adequate nutrition comes, in large measure, from the national condition of unemployment. There are just too few jobs to go around now and in the future there will be even more people looking for work that does not exist. Masses of hungry unemployed people provide a very fertile bed for the seeds of revolution. In our urban centers the problems of overpopulation have gone beyond the point where they can be ignored and, according to some experts, beyond the point where they can be solved. It is fast coming to the stage where urban areas will be inhabited only by the very wealthy and the very poor. An arrested population growth would possibly give public and private builders a chance to fill the housing needs of all social classes in time to save our cities.

Some people see the movement of the middle class to the suburbs as a good thing because it creates a forced decentralization of population thereby taking the pressure off the cities. This is a pipe dream. Suburbanites are absentee polluters of our cities. The automobiles which they rely upon were manufactured near urban centers in factories whose smoke stacks polluted the air over those cities. The gasoline burned by suburban two-car families was derived from crude petroleum cracked in plants that send noxious fumes into the air over various urban centers. The goods they consume were also made in urban industrial complexes. In essence, suburban people, especially those who look around at their wide open spaces and assume they can have as many children as they like because conditions of overcrowding do not exist in their communities, are creating problems for the cities and then divorcing themselves from those problems by moving away. And they go one step further. They make it more difficult for urban centers to tackle their problems because suburbanites earn their money in the city and spend it on goods and services and taxes outside the city. This removes a great deal of revenue that municipal governments need to combat the difficulties of overpopulation and to improve urban facilities.

Ultimately those people who swim to the suburbs to spawn will find that the problems of overpopulation have reached their doorsteps. Dr. Paul Ehrlich discusses this in his article, "World Population: Is the Battle Lost?"

> Some men doubtless profit from the economic effects of a growing population, and are able to retreat from riot-torn cities to the increasingly smoggy countryside in order to live. But what kind of world will their children inherit—social disorder and unemployment on an unprecedented scale? Will they have to wear smog masks as a matter of routine? Will they enjoy mock steaks made from processed grass or seaweed? . . . Above all, will they be able to retain their sanity in a world gone mad?*

It is time that we Americans faced the fact that there is no place to hide from the negative effects of natalism. It is also time that our middle and upper classes shouldered some of the responsibility and stopped blaming the poor. The truth is that none of us, rich or poor, black or white can afford to reproduce in the future as we have done in the past. True, very poor people do make economic demands on society, but by the same token, monied people make demands on the environment. The automobile emissions that cloud cities in unhealthy smog, the jet planes whose exhaust fouls the upper atmosphere and

* Paul R. Ehrlich, "World Population: Is the Battle Lost?" *Stanford Today* (Winter 1968, Series 1, no. 22).

whose engines contribute to noise pollution, and the mountains of junk and garbage generated by our affluent society are burdens our ecological system cannot continue to carry. Large families, no matter what economic class they belong to, must be discouraged if any of us are to survive.

With all the problems both at home and abroad created by overpopulation why do many people still insist on having large families? There are no simple answers to this but the Population Reference Bureau does make an attempt to deal with the question by listing seven of the most common "pronatalist" influences. These are: 1. the belief among men and women that procreation leads to self-fulfillment and provides a way of achieving immortality; 2. the notion among women that having many children provides a way of finding the self-actualization denied them by lack of interesting employment opportunities; 3. the fact that many poor families are unable to receive adequate birth control counseling; 4. the efforts made by certain families to achieve a certain sex distribution among their children; 5. the "growthmania" that afflicts certain Americans and makes them believe that population growth is both necessary and good for the economy; 6. the policies of our government that foster large families through tax deductions for children and public assistance for families who cannot meet their own needs; and 7. the relative lack of information from the government and the mass media telling people of the grave dangers of overpopulation.*

* *Population Bulletin*, vol. XXVI, No. 1, April 1970, pp. 25-26.

The first two pronatal influences simply underscore the wrong reasons for parenthood already discussed, but the third pronatal influence, the unavailability of birth control counseling for poor people, can only be countered by massive government effort on the local, state, and national levels. Contraception clinics staffed by professionals and informed laymen should be established in the communities where they are needed and should provide not only counseling but also birth control devices to people who cannot afford them. The cost of running such clinics would in the long run be offset by a decrease in the public relief rolls. As a stopgap measure it would be a good idea to have mobile contraception clinics somewhat like the mobile units that provide free chest x-rays for tuberculosis diagnosis. In addition, those states which permit abortions should have programs that provide the operation on an ability-to-pay basis. Women whose family income is below a specified level would receive free abortions while those with higher incomes would pay an amount determined by their income level.

Far and away the most foolish pronatalistic influence is the attempt made by some families to achieve a desired sex distribution among their children. A good parent will love a boy or girl infant equally well. Even if a couple has a definite preference, breeding until a child of the desired sex is born is still not the answer. If, after having two children, they still wish an additional child of a particular sex, they should adopt. Aside from limiting family size, this is the only way they can be sure of guaranteeing their choice.

The fifth pronatalistic influence, "growthmania," is an

anachronism. At one time our country did need more children to assure continued economic growth. But that time has long since passed. Unfortunately our government's tax structure is still designed to encourage the birth rate—the sixth pronatalistic influence. Single people and childless couples in our country are taxed at the higher rates although they use fewer of the government's services than families with children who require more of the various local, state, and national government services. While this does not mean that people can expect to grow rich from having children, it does mean that the government helps to offset the costs of having and raising children. Furthermore, the government policy of providing increased economic aid to welfare families who have additional children also creates an atmosphere that works against effective population control. Some experts have proposed the idea of taxing couples who exceed the two-per-family guideline while others talk about doing away with all income tax deductions for children. To avoid directing such measures against the poor, they would have to be instituted on a graduated basis. However, it would be an effective way of putting people on notice that if they want the luxury of a large family they are going to have to pay for it. Regarding welfare it would be unjust to penalize children by lowering their family relief budget because their parents continue to increase their number of brothers and sisters, but the idea of paying welfare recipients incentives to have abortions or sterilization operations, on a voluntary basis, might work.

A less desirable governmental method has been suggested by Hawaii's State Senator Nadao Yoshinaga who introduced a bill in the Hawaiian legislature calling for the compulsory sterilization of women after the birth of their second child. Such legislation may be the harbinger of the world George Orwell wrote about in his book *1984*. Such intrusions into personal freedom are a natural outgrowth of overpopulation. To prevent such an eventuality the government should start taking an active hand now to discourage large families on a voluntary basis.

The seventh and final pronatal influence is the relative lack of information and propaganda from the mass media telling people about the dangers of unrestricted family size. In the past months many private organizations have sponsored anti-smoking commercials on television which have helped two million Americans to quit smoking. If the same type of campaign were launched against large families perhaps two million Americans would decide not to have more than two children. This at least would be a start in solving the problem of overpopulation.

A pronatal influence that the Population Reference Bureau does not mention deals with those militants who actively promote the idea of having big families among members of their particular ethnic or racial groups by saying that family planning and limitation are really thinly disguised plots by the establishment to commit genocide. This line of thinking is both paranoid and self-defeating. Richard A. Watson and Philip M. Smith state that the chaos caused by overpopulation might lead to genocide:

> If this occurs it is possible that one of the major national powers will then impose totalitarian control over the rest of the world. And if overpopulation is seen to be

the cause of the world's ills, those who rule a world government by conquest will probably reduce the world's population efficiently, but not necessarily in the fairest and most humane way.*

Those who fear the elimination of their ethnic or racial group by government may be converting those fears into reality by insisting that their people have large families.

The two questions that now come up are: "What can we expect if we do make that start?" and "How do we go about making it?" Representative Udall provides some answers:

Suppose I told you that I have a plan which would guarantee to every area of the country: reduced local, state and Federal taxes; less crowded streets, freeways and hospitals; single-session schools and shortened waiting lists at colleges; some genuine hope for lowered crime rates; measurable progress against pollution. This plan would cost almost nothing in public spending and involve no government controls. Under it, you might wake up each morning to a newspaper filled with heartening progress rather than the calamity of the day.

Well, I have such a plan. I can't be optimistic that it will be adopted very soon, but it ought to be. Here it is:

Americans, voluntarily and openly, must face the fact that many of our tensions and failures are due to a spiraling population growth. Every family with two

* Richard A. Watson and Philip M. Smith, "The Limit: 500 Million," *Focus/Midwest* (vol. 8, no. 51), p. 42.

*or more children would make a personal, voluntary
decision to have no more. Every couple with one child
or none would agree to stop with the second.**

This is an effective solution that puts no one to a great
deal of trouble or expense. And there is no question that
if we do not adopt a voluntary curb, the government will
eventually be forced to take steps that will gradually
erode our traditional American freedoms. Zero Population Growth's Judy Senderowtiz explains what can and
will happen to the American way of life if people insist
on having large families:

. . . democracy obviously doesn't work when there are
too many people. . . . If you look at the little town
meetings of the early Massachusetts Bay colonies you'll
see that everyone who had something to say was lis-
tened to. They had a real form of democracy because
the population was small enough so that individual
views mattered and were taken into consideration. . . .
Now we have a representative for every X number of
people and as the population increases that representative will have more constituents in his district. . . .
How can a representative or a senator possibly listen
to all those people? They can't.
. . . and overpopulation will limit our freedoms.
There is a very definite positive correlation between
numbers of people and numbers of rules and regulations. All kinds of licensing, controls, and restrictive
laws increase as the population increases.

* Morris K. Udall, "Standing Room Only on Spaceship Earth,"
Arizona Magazine (July 27, 1969).

If we look to the future, a future where our population has perhaps doubled, it becomes clear that the government would have to limit personal freedoms in order to maintain some kind of social order. Let us consider some of the rights we take for granted today and see what could conceivably happen to them.

The right of unrestricted travel: When our streets and highways become so crowded that no vehicle can move, the government will have to begin issuing travel permits to limit the numbers of people on the road at any given time. This would mean that a person planning a trip would have to apply to some government bureau for permission to use certain roads during a specified time period. The old idea of picking up and going off to the mountains or seashore would be a thing of the past.

The right to live where you want: Families who wish to move to certain areas may find they are unable to do so because those areas have been declared overpopulated and closed to newcomers. Then these families will have put their names on waiting lists and hope that someone will move out so that they can move in. And of course government agencies might be set up to determine if certain overcrowded areas required forced emigration as a way of relieving their problems.

The right to eat what you want: As the ability of the land available for cultivation decreases in its ability to feed our multitudes, the Department of Agriculture might be forced to order farmers to raise only those crops that have the most nutritional qualities and require the least growing space. This would mean that people would have to be satisfied with certain staple foods rather than a varied and interesting diet. Meat may also be rationed because cattle require too much land for grazing.

The right to an education of your choosing: When educational facilities become unable to handle the numbers of students applying for admission, a national system of student selection may be instituted. Based on a series of aptitude tests candidates will be given the option of training only for what they seem most suited, even if they have little interest in that field, or of not going to school at all. Overcrowded high schools, colleges, and graduate schools will not have the flexibility to allow students to choose their own majors nor will they be able to permit students to change their minds about their selection of courses after they have begun studying. It will be a case of either learn what the government wants you to learn or learn nothing at all.

The right to have children: There may come a time in the future when the government may have to take drastic steps to curb the population growth and this could involve the removal of the right of some people to have any children at all. For example, certain government-selected groups might be permanently sterilized. Less dramatically, all couples who have two children might be sterilized. If you think this is far-fetched, remember that it is beginning to happen in India. John W. Dykstra, associate professor of science at Jersey City College, says in his article, "Imperative: Education for Reproductive Responsibility":

In those nations that fail to educate their peoples effectively concerning national population needs, an increas-

115

ing amount of coercive governmental intervention in the determination of family size can be anticipated. Compulsory sterilization or imprisonment are the likely fate of those who jeopardize the future of their society through an irresponsible incidence of reproduction. A bill providing for the sterilization of those males with three or more children was introduced last year in the Indian parliament. Some Indian states now provide a sum of money to those who volunteer to be sterilized. . . . If present research efforts are successful, the vaccination of a population against pregnancy during most of their fertile life will be another measure available to governments.*

To people who say they want to have large families because they claim to love children we ask: Is this the kind of world you want your children to live in? A world where governments tamper with their biological systems, control their personal lives, and regulate their everyday activities. A world in which they will breathe filthy air, drink polluted water loaded with chemical purifiers, and eventually lose their human qualities as they are forced to push and fight each other for the last bit of space or the last morsel of food. Or do you want them to live in a world that provides all the freedoms, all the space, and all the opportunities that will make their lives worthwhile? The choice must be made *now* and for people who love children that choice should be a simple one.

For many people, talking about the broad ecological, social, and political consequences of natalism is meaning-

* John W. Dykstra, "Imperative: Education for Reproductive Responsibility," *Phi Beta Kappan*, May, 1968, pp. 505-506.

less. Parents often fail to understand, or fail to *want* to understand, how their children could possibly contribute to the creation of anything as monstrous as the world we have discussed. For others, primarily those parents in suburban or rural areas, overpopulation is not yet real enough for them to seriously consider. They look around and see green lawns, trees, and plenty of open space for their children to play in and wonder what all the environmental hubbub is about.

However, many such parents, though not impressed with seemingly abstract eventualities, can understand that their own children will have a better life in a small family. Overwhelmingly, social scientists, child psychologists, and family relations experts are saying that small families are happier and more crisis-free than big families; that children with only one brother or sister tend to be smarter and more creative than those with many siblings; and that parents with fewer children have a much better chance of attaining personal self-fulfillment and achieving economic security. Having a small family, choosing quality over quantity, is a very pragmatic way to assure the best possible life-style for both parents and children.

Children with only one or two siblings have a much greater chance of achieving success in school because small-family life fosters mental development. In his *New York Times Magazine* article, "The Case for Small Families," psychiatrist Dr. E. James Lieberman describes some recent findings:

> Scientists are also finding that the small-family child is superior in a number of ways to his large-family counterpart:

Brighter: About 70 percent of the draftees rejected on tests for mental ability come from families of four or more children. And 47 percent of these rejectees belong to families with six or more children.

It could be argued that, because many of these families are poor, poverty rather than family size is the culprit. However, a careful study done in Scotland showed that the number of children in the family affects intelligence at each economic level. Children from small families consistently outscored those from big families in the same income bracket.

More creative: Teen-age boys judged to be most creative in the annual Westinghouse Science Talent Search usually come from two-child families, only rarely from larger ones.*

There are several reasons why small-family children are brighter. The most obvious is that parents of one or two children have more time to help in their learning processes and often are better able to afford intellectual aids such as encyclopedias, creative toys, and trips to places of educational interest. And, of course, homes with fewer children where students can have their own quiet corner or room are more conducive to study. Furthermore, small-family parents are better able to individualize their children's specific learning difficulties and to cope with them personally, by enlisting the teacher's aid, or by hiring a tutor. Large-family parents are often hampered by finances or infant children who require 'round-the-

* E. James Lieberman, "The Case for Small Families, *New York Times Magazine*, p. 86.

clock care. In our experiences as teachers in the New York City school system we found that small-family parents were the most likely to come to school to discuss their children's problems. Large-family parents often could not spare the time.

We mentioned earlier that the average middle-class family can expect to spend somewhere in the neighborhood of $25,000 to $30,000, excluding college, in raising each of their children. And it is rapidly coming to the point in our country where a college education is the minimum requirement for an interesting and well-paying job. In many large middle-class families parents must choose who will and who will not go to college. The most frequent decision is to send the sons and not the daughters. Another discriminatory practice is to send the older children.

Creativity in children often requires special attention to be brought to full bloom. In the first place it must be noticed, and noticing creative talent in one's own children is not as easy as it sounds. How many times have you heard the parents of college age men and women react with total surprise when their child suddenly changes his major from teaching, business administration, or mathematics to art, creative writing, or drama? "I didn't know he was interested in the arts," they say, "and I never knew he was gifted."

In small families the exceptional gifts children may possess are more likely to be noticed than in big families simply because small-family parents know their children more intimately. Parents with large broods frequently handle their children in a quantitative manner which means they only pay attention to those abilities that can be given a numerical value on a report card. The subtleties of creativity often escape a simple A-B-C grading. Once spotted, childhood creativity should be developed either through private lessons or special schools or camps. And usually this means money, money that small families are more likely to have available than large families.

No doubt there are very creative children who come from large families, but they are the exception and not the rule. On the whole, creativity is a flower that flourishes best where it is not crowded, unnoticed, and uncared for.

Along with superior intellectual and creative qualities, small families also tend to develop children whose emotional adjustment is better than average. This reflects the fact that small-family homes are generally more democratic and accepting of individual idiosyncracies. Parents of large families, like governments of large populations, must rely on a great many rules and regulations to maintain order, and this can have a negative effect on a child's psychological development. Wayne H. Holtzman and Bernice Milburn Moore in their study, "Family Structure and Youth Attitudes," present some of the less desirable emotional qualities that children from large families exhibit:

> Youth from the largest families, with six to nine children or more, were consistently more negativistic and less egalitarian in their attitudes. They were the most pessimistic about the world and its people. They were distrustful of relationships with others. For them, authoritarian discipline was more often accepted as the

"better way." Criticism of education was more prevalent among them. . . . Family tensions were also recognized as high among members of such large households.*

Children from large families whose parents use authoritarian controls are often not very self-reliant and tend to require great amounts of teacher approval in order to feel secure in a classroom situation. This relates directly to their home lives and the leader-dependent relationship they have established with their parents. As we have said, authoritarian parents give their children virtually no opportunity to learn how to make their own decisions or to express their preferences. Such children generally require highly structured surroundings in which their every activity is preplotted because their parent-dominated upbringing offered them little training in organizing their own activities. It is also characteristic of authoritarian parents to rely on obvious methods of approval and disapproval. Although democratic mothers and fathers also use such methods, they frequently permit their children to evaluate their own behavior. This affords democratically reared children the chance to develop a personal sense of right and wrong against which they can compare their actions, an attribute not often fostered in large families.

The child with few brothers and sisters has yet one

* Wayne H. Holtzman and Bernice Milburn Moore, "Family Structure and Youth Attitudes," *Problems of Youth: Transition to Adulthood in a Changing World*, eds. Muzafer Sherif and Carolyn W. Sherif, Aldine Publishing Company (Chicago, 1965), p. 52.

more edge over the child with many siblings and that is in terms of physical development. Dr. Lieberman says that children from small families are:

> *Bigger and taller*: A British scientist found that as families grew larger, the average height and weight for each child decreased. Although the big-family babies had normal weights at birth, by school age they had not attained the growth of their small-family contemporaries.*

Not only do children from small families tend to grow bigger and taller, but they are also less likely to suffer physical abuse. The "battered-child syndrome" is more and more widely recognized now that many states have passed laws allowing doctors, school nurses, teachers, and other professionals to report suspected cases of child abuse without jeopardizing themselves. Of course, the percentage of parents who beat their children beyond the point of reason is fractional, nonetheless this situation does exist and it does affect many children. In 1969 there were 50,000 cases of child abuse reported in the United States and that figure is probably low because many cases are suppressed.

There are two major reasons why parents physically abuse their children: 1. individual personality problems; and 2. problems within the marriage relationship. In either case an incident is usually only triggered by severe crisis. Dr. Henry Haberfeld of New York City's Task Force on Child Abuse says:

* E. James Lieberman, "The Case for Small Families," *New York Times Magazine*, p. 86.

If you're asking does a crisis situation in the family have an impact on the likelihood of an abuse situation occurring, the answer is definitely yes. Family crises is one of the ingredients that goes into it. And indeed the commonest and the most frequent crisis is another pregnancy . . . certainly an unwanted pregnancy or a pregnancy at a bad time.

There can be no doubt that in certain large families there are already unplanned-for children whom the parents have neither the economic nor the emotional resources to provide for. News of yet another unwanted pregnancy may be the final pressure leading to a battered child. One way of avoiding such tragedies would be for mothers and fathers to space their children so that the arrival of a new baby will be the blessed event it should be rather than the beginning of financial privation, increased family tensions, and unreasoned physical punishment of children who committed no crime other than being born.

We mentioned earlier that the average middle-class family can expect to spend somewhere in the neighborhood of $25,000 to $30,000, excluding college, in raising each of their children. And it is rapidly coming to the point in our country where a college education is a necessity. In the super-technical world of the future, the world today's children will be living in, a higher education, along with food, clothing, and shelter, will be an essential for survival. Families who can afford to send their children to college will be doing a lot to assure their sons and daughters of having the first choice of employment opportunities while parents who cannot afford a higher education for their children will be assuring them of the second choice of the left-over jobs.

In many large middle-class families a kind of discrimination takes place in regard to deciding who will and who will not go to college. The most frequent is the tendency of big-family parents to send sons rather than daughters. This is most unfortunate because the role of women in the future, both as career people and as mothers and wives, will demand an intellectually developed mind. The second discriminatory practice of large families is reflected in the fact that first and second born children more often go on to higher education than their brothers and sisters who come along a little later in the family birth order. While many variables play a part in this, economics cannot be discounted. In many cases certain large-family children are denied college and university educations simply because the family budget cannot support another student. On the other hand, by having a small family parents increase their financial ability to provide an equal opportunity for excellence for all of their children.

Any discussion of family size must take into account the fears that many parents have in regard to raising an only child. In truth most of these fears are groundless. They are based on inaccurate studies that set out to prove the preconceived idea that only children tend to be below average in school achievement, selfish, lacking in personal control, and prone to physical ill health. Objective investigation has shown these findings to be false. In his doctoral dissertation titled "The Only Child in the Family: A Comparison With Other Orders of Birth," William Paul Carter clearly states:

> In the studies of college students no significant differences were found between only children and others on nearly all tests in regard to emotional stability, neurotic tendencies, physical development, health, scholarship, and several other personality traits.*

And Dorothy Tunell Dyer in her article, "Are Only Children Different?" goes one step further by saying that in certain personality traits, only children may be somewhat superior to non-onlies:

> Only children at the college level seem to be as well adjusted as non-only children, when the total scores of the Bell Adjustment Inventory are compared for woman students. In the Home Area of the Bell Adjustment the only children showed a somewhat better adjustment and in the Emotional Area the slight difference favors the only child.**

If indeed only children *do* face problems in growing up these problems are more likely to be caused by their parents rather than by their lack of brothers and sisters. James E. Bossard and Eleanor Boll in their book, *Family Situations*, explain why this is so:

* William Paul Carter, "The Only Child in the Family: A Comparison With Other Orders of Birth." A dissertation submitted to the Faculty of the Division of the Social Sciences in Candidacy of Ph.D. of Sociology. Department of Sociology, University of Chicago, 1937.

** Dorothy Tunell Dyer, "Are Only Children Different?" *Journal of Educational Psychology*, vol. 36, April 1945, p. 301.

These conclusions, summed up and considered in the light of the family situation alone, are that the differences between large and small families are chiefly one of degree. Whatever the family is like, the only child within it receives the concentrated force of all its influences. If the parents are over-attentive he gets more over-attention than if he had siblings. If they are under-attentive, then he is lonelier.*

Parents who, for economic or personal reasons, would like to have only one child but fear that their child will suffer as a result of being an only can lay their apprehensions aside by realizing that it is their capabilities as parents, and not the number of children in the family, that will ultimately be responsible for the quality of the development of their child. And if their concern centers about their child not having a companion to grow up with, family relations specialist Dr. Rebecca Liswood has these words of advice:

> People say that if they have only one child, that child would not have a companion. . . . I think that's a mistaken notion. If you want a companion for your child you can invite over other children of your child's age. People must realize that brothers and sisters are not necessarily companions. First of all, except for twins, there are bound to be age differences. And in the second place, many siblings tend to view each other as rivals rather than friends.

* James H. S. Bossard and Eleanor S. Boll, *Family Situations*, copyright 1943, University of Pennsylvania Press and reprinted by Greenwood Press, Publishers, N.Y., p. 158.

Parents who are capable of recognizing and dealing with the special needs of only children may actually be doing their child a service by *not* bringing additional children into the family. Says Dr. John E. Horrocks, author of *The Psychology of Adolescence*:

> As a matter of fact there are advantages in being an only child. Studies have shown that, particularly in the case of girls, only children tend to be more precocious in many of the aspects of language development. Such children have an opportunity of greater association with adults and greater opportunities to acquire and practice the skills essential for participation in non-child centered situations. Parental affection need not be divided and sibling rivalry is absent. . . . He (the only child) has the rare privilege of privacy so often impossible in large families.*

By limiting the size of their family, parents would not only be doing a beautiful thing for their children but they would also be doing some wonderful things for themselves. Mothers and fathers of one or two children have a greater chance for self-actualization, emotional and marital happiness, economic security, and physical good health than parents who are subjected to the psychological and physical stresses of large numbers of children.

We have all heard about those big-family parents who worked and slaved so that their children would have enough to eat and sufficient clothing to wear, and perhaps the chance to go to college. These devoted parents

* John E. Horrocks, *The Psychology of Adolscence*, Houghton Mifflin Company, Boston, 1962, p. 110.

spent whatever money they earned to raise their children and had little left over for their own needs and pleasures. It can be argued that their eventual rewards came when their sons graduated from college and when their daughters married well. No doubt this was some compensation for all those long and hard years. But many of today's parents are realizing that by having small families they can have the pleasure of seeing their children succeed as well as the pleasure of enjoying their own lives. The economic demands of small families are usually not so harsh as to prohibit parents from going out for an evening's entertainment, taking vacations, and buying those "little extras" that make life so much more pleasant. If you want to lead an economically well-balanced life where you as parents can share in the pie, then a small family is the answer.

Mothers and fathers who limit the number of their children tend to be emotionally more stable and experience fewer marital problems. Says Dr. Lieberman:

> It has been fairly well established that each additional child creates more friction between husband and wife as well as between parents and offspring. . . . Scientists have reported that parents of large families suffer more mental and physical illnesses than those who head small ones. Our statisticians at the National Institute of Mental Health say that adults with four or more children are more likely to be patients in mental hospitals, too.*

* E. James Lieberman, "The Case for Small Families," *New York Times Magazine*, p. 86.

It does not require much digging to discover the reasons for this. Mothers with a great number of howling infants, demanding pre-schoolers, mischievous school-agers, and impossible adolescents often find that they are taxed to the point of mental and physical exhaustion. And large-family fathers who must work overtime or hold two jobs at once to support their wives and many children, only to come home at day's end to a noisy house filled with discipline problems, are highly susceptible to physical and psychological illness.

Not only do the strains of large-family life increase the possibility of illness for mothers, but the frequency of childbirth and the lack of child spacing also plays a big part in adversely affecting their physical well-being. Obstetrician-gynecologist Dr. O. J. Miller talks about a frequently occurring medical problem faced by mothers who have too many children too close together:

> Many women, particularly those who don't have a good diet or who don't follow the doctor's advice, are going to have an iron deficiency anemia as a result of the demands of the fetus on the internal iron stores. So that if she has frequent pregnancies, this is going to be a larger demand on iron. This is one very definite effect of very close pregnancies.

The weight of evidence continues to build, tipping the scales more and more in favor of the small family. Behavioral scientists, ecologists, physicians, economists, and politicians are all telling us in no uncertain terms that the old "cheaper by the dozen" attitude toward child-bearing must be abandoned.

V

Marriages
Without Children

Along with the Myth of Maternal Instinct people have been brainwashed for centuries by the Myth of Family Instinct, the belief that men and women seek one another for the purpose not just of mating, but of setting up house and raising children. There is, of course, a good deal of seemingly valid evidence to support this notion because all cultures have some kind of basic social institution that can be called a family, monogamous or otherwise. However, most anthropologists and sociologists believe that the desire for family life does not spring from some internal biological source, but rather from the following four external pressures: 1. the need to provide a socially workable way for frequent sexual satisfaction; 2. the need to provide a means of caring for the elderly; 3. the need for a convenient method of insuring food, clothing, and shelter; and 4. the need for an institution to care for and educate children.

No one has to be an expert in the field of marital relations to see that these four basic motivations for family life have been drastically modified in recent years. And as the needs of men and women within a society change, the nature of social institutions must also change if they are to remain relevant. Throughout history, the family *has* survived largely because of its dynamic ability to adjust to drastic cultural change. One of the most radical shifts in socio-cultural behavior resulted when the Industrial Revolution induced thousands of families to leave their farms for urban centers. In the cities couples were hard pressed to find adequate living space for themselves and their children let alone grandparents. Many people thought that without the older folks in the home the meaning of family life would be lost. But despite its drawbacks, the nuclear family—husband, wife, and children—continues to thrive while grandparents, with the aid of job pensions, social security, and perhaps some help from their children, have managed to make their own way. Urbanization also put an end to the family as a self-reliant economic unit. In a rural setting family members depended on each other for survival, but in the city they were forced to turn to strangers—landlords, grocers, and clothing merchants. Fathers, and frequently mothers, had to leave the home to earn money to purchase these necessities. Even in the face of such changes, the family unit persisted.

Of more recent concern is the current sexual revolution. Historically most societies have forgiven adulterous males while severely condemning the straying wife. Studies show that while the large majority of married men have at least one extramarital affair, only about 25 percent of married women have been unfaithful. If the new sexual mores grant women the same moral dispensations as men, will the family suffer? Sociologist Dr. Joseph K. Folsom believes that it will not:

> The typical coitus is a repetition of the act with a familiar individual rather than a casual or varietist act; "promiscuity" never applies to most of the people for most of the time.*

If wives begin to have affairs as many husbands do, then the institution of marriage will have to adapt.

In regard to its childrearing functions, the family has already changed a good deal. Families are considerably smaller today than they were in the early part of the twentieth century. Still, most people equate family life with having children and until very recently few people have dared to question the widely held idea that a marriage is improved by having children.

Before discussing the validity of this concept, let us consider the most common reasons why couples choose to remain childless.

The most extensive study of the reasons that married couples remained childless which we were able to find was done back in 1936 by Dr. Paul Popenoe who examined the case histories of 862 childless couples.** Two

---

* Joseph K. Folsom, "Sexual and Affectional Functions of the Family," *The Encyclopedia of Sexual Behavior*, Albert Ellis and Albert Abarbanel, eds. (2nd edition), Hawthorne Books, Inc., New York City, p. 394.

** Paul Popenoe, "Motivations of Childless Marriages," *Journal of Heredity*, vol. 27, 1936, pp. 469-472.

generalizations resulting from his investigation were that almost one out of every five educated white American couples were childless and that only one third of the couples in his sample had been unable to conceive. This is an interesting bit of information because it suggests that educated men and women are more likely to seek alternative life-styles to parenthood. Furthermore, it dispels the notion that most childless marriages result from sterility of the husband or wife.

The following seven motivations for childless marriages, adapted from Dr. Popenoe's study, should help explain why some people feel they are better off without children.

Self-centered This heading was not chosen to indicate selfishness, but as Popenoe explains, for lack of a better term to describe husbands and wives who feel that children would interfere with their way of living.

Many couples believe that having children would prevent them from doing the things they find most enjoyable. Husbands and wives who like to travel, pursue active social lives, or involve themselves in community or political matters might, indeed, find children very restricting.

Under this motive for childless marriages Popenoe also includes those couples who are ". . . so much in love with each other that they couldn't bear to think of children that might come between them and spoil the perfection of their romance." This is not an unwarranted fear. Marriage counselors recognize the fact that children do come between parents to the extent that mothers must divide their affections between their children and their husbands.

While many people feel that children make their marriage complete, there are a good number of couples who feel psychologically satisfied with their relationship and consider parenthood unnecessary. Their happiness lies in pursuing their mutual interests, following their personal inclinations, and in enjoying each other as individuals without diluting that enjoyment with additional family members. Some people may consider such couples as selfish because they refuse to share their happiness with a child, but this is a far less dangerous brand of selfishness than that of couples who become parents hoping that children will give their marriage a purpose.

Wife's career The second most frequent motivation for not having children is that some wives feel childbearing will restrict their careers. In other words, these women feel free to choose alternatives to motherhood. In his interviews Dr. Popenoe discovered one possibly surprising fact: the employed wives appeared to share a closer personal relationship with their husbands than the wives who stayed at home. One reason is that a woman with a career of her own has a great deal more in common with her spouse. Their interests are similar and they can communicate with each other as equals. For some marriages the uninterrupted employment of the wife could be the thing that keeps the relationship alive.

Economic pressure Dr. Popenoe notes that this classification is ". . . intended to take only those cases where husband and wife could not afford children—not those in which they preferred to be childless and rationalized this emotional attitude by explaining that they didn't want to have a child until they were sure they could give them every advantage . . ."

We feel that Dr. Popenoe should also have included in his study such couples who may not have been rationalizing at all but honestly facing financial facts. For example, a couple living on two incomes might realistically decide that the loss of the wife's paycheck plus the additional cost of raising a child, while not putting them in the poorhouse, would definitely mean that they would not be able to give their child the quality of life to which they feel he is entitled. This cannot be dismissed as a rationalization.

The childless couples that Popenoe *does* include are those who face financial hardship either because the husband is unable to work or because both husband and wife must help support an elderly parent or a physically or mentally handicapped brother or sister.

Health   This motivation for childlessness is self-obvious. Certain women may have physical problems that would be aggravated by pregnancy or birth while others may have a disease that could hurt the child either prenatally or postnatally.

Dislike of children   Surprisingly this reason for avoiding parenthood comprised only 8 percent of Dr. Popenoe's study, although it would appear the most logical explanation for remaining childless. Not everyone is thrilled by infants, marvels when a baby first says

Mama or Da-Da, or enjoys answering a child's endless stream of questions. However, the social pressures against verbalizing such attitudes are great. Women and, to a lesser degree, men are supposed to love children and most are afraid to admit they don't.

In truth, dislike of children is a broad heading that can be divided into six more specific reasons for avoiding parenthood.

1. *Plain dislike.* For some people children are more a source of annoyance and distraction than of pleasure. They feel that the joys of parenthood are just too few to compensate for the responsibility, trouble, and cost of rearing a child. In short, these people just have not acquired a taste for children and the children they have come in contact with—nephews, nieces, and neighbors' kids—did nothing to stimulate their appetites.

2. *Neurotic dislike.* This subheading includes those people who fear they will not like their children because they were neglected by their own parents. This may be classified as an abstract fear rather than a concrete dislike of children and it is not terribly valid since it is based on illogical apprehensions that might never come to pass.

3. *Dislike of pregnancy.* Advertisements for maternity clothes try to sell women on the idea that they can be both beautiful and pregnant. And many girls *do* feel that a woman is never more beautiful than when she is pregnant. However, some ladies just do not buy this idea while others fear their looks will be permanently marred as a result of pregnancy. Then too, many husbands do not look forward either to their wives having bulging bellies or to the curtailment of sexual intercourse that

pregnancy may cause. For these couples, the ultimate reward of having a child is in no way justified by the discomforts and inconveniences.

4. *Dislike of childbearing.* There are women who have a justifiable fear of childbearing because they have some physical problem that would make delivery difficult. Others are simply too afraid of delivery to desire pregnancy, often recalling a close friend or relative who suffered greatly or even died as a result of giving birth. In this case some professional counseling is advisable so that a couple who truly desire children will not deny themselves parenthood because of a groundless fear.

5. *Eugenics* Among those married couples whose families have histories of inherited mental or physical illness there is concern that their own children will also suffer from these afflictions. However, this concern should not *necessarily* turn to fear. Amram Scheinfeld, in his book *The Basic Facts of Human Heredity* discusses the problem:

> The most common of the personal heredity problems involve fear of inheritance or transmission of defects, diseases or other undesirable traits. In each case, once it is clear that a given condition is hereditary, decisions must be governed by its severity; the nature of its inheritance and the risk of transmission; the stage of life at which it appears; the degree of its interference with happiness, work or adjustment; and how prepared parents might be to have and rear a child so afflicted.*

* Amram Scheinfeld, *The Basic Facts of Human Heredity*, 1961, Washington Square Press, New York City, p. 238.

The best thing for couples facing such a decision to do is to consult a physician who specializes in genetics. His opinion should be the determining factor as to whether or not they should try to conceive. In the event that there *is* a great likelihood that the defect will appear, the couple should then consider adoption.

6. *Marital discord*   One of the wrong reasons for parenthood that we discussed earlier dealt with unhappy couples who hoped children would save their floundering marriages. Psychologists and marriage counselors are opposed to this concept because the presence of children often makes it more difficult for husband and wife to work out their difficulties and, in the event of divorce, it is the child who suffers most.

Although many people concede that certain couples would be better off if they did not become parents, few believe that a childless marriage can be as stable or as emotionally satisfying as one that has produced offspring. Statistics indicate that childless marriages have a higher incidence of divorce and some studies have concluded that there is a positive correlation between marital happiness and childbearing. However, more recent and more extensive investigations have shown that these earlier findings are either questionable or false.

What the earlier studies failed to take into account is that simply because two things co-exist—in this case divorce and childlessness—it does not necessarily mean that a cause and effect relationship also exists. Thomas Monahan, in his article, "Is Childlessness Related to Family Stability?" concludes:

The statistical evidence produced in this article should serve to show that the alleged association between divorce and childlessness has been a statistically spurious one and may not exist at all.*

Sociologist Ray E. Baber agrees, laying to rest the belief that married people are playing Russian Roulette with the divorce statistics if they fail to become parents:

It is unsafe to say that childlessness causes divorce. Perhaps it does in a few cases, but most of the relationship is probably due to other factors. One is that the peak of divorce now comes during the second year of marriage, with the first and third years almost as high. This fact, coupled with the growing tendency to postpone children until a few years after marriage, accounts for many of the childless divorces. Marital troubles frequently come before the couple is ready for children, and the very fact of their seeming incompatibility makes them postpone children still longer, until they see how their marriage is going to turn out.**

Actually, the truth of the matter is that *divorce can cause childlessness*. The significance of this realization for the case against having children is twofold: First, as we have frequently repeated, couples in marital difficulty should remain childless until their problems are ironed out one way or the other. And second, young couples

* Thomas Monahan, "Is Childlessness Related to Family Stability?" *American Sociological Review*, 1955, 20, p. 456.
** Ray E. Baber, *Marriage and the Family*, 2nd edition, 1953, McGraw-Hill Book Company, Inc., New York, p. 504.

should not jump into parenthood until they have had a few years to decide if their marriage is going the way they would like it to go. It may be terribly unromantic to say "We are waiting to have children until we're sure that we will stay together," but the cold fact that one marriage in three goes on the rocks must be faced. Not only does the presence of children in a troubled marriage make it more difficult for husband and wife to overcome their problems but children also may lock two people into a relationship that neither wants.

An interesting sidelight to the question of marital stability and childbearing is the fact that desertions occur more frequently in marriages where there are children.* Husbands, who do most of the deserting, are more inclined to leave a wife and children than a wife alone for several reasons.

In most desertion cases, family finances play a big part. A husband who is unable to live up to his expected role as breadwinner may feel so emasculated that he decides to disappear. In other cases a husband seeking public assistance may find that his family is ineligible because he is employed and living at home. Believing that his wife and children would be better off on a welfare grant than on his wages, he also deserts.

In some cases the birth of a child itself may encourage desertion. For example, a husband or wife who feels emotionally shortchanged because their spouse pays too much attention to the baby may desert in an attempt to find a more gratifying relationship. And then there are those

* Monahan, p. 456.

individuals who are frightened by the responsibilities of parenthood and simply run away.

Whatever the reason for the relationship between child-bearing and desertion, one thing should be perfectly clear: Children are no guarantee that a couple will stay together and, as Monahan states, "Marital stability, in the final analysis, may have no general relationship to childbearing."*

The general belief that the arrival of a child, especially the first, marks the beginning of true marital happiness, is not borne out by the facts. A study of the psychological reactions of 46 young middle-class couples to the arrival of the first child was carried out by E. E. LeMasters. He found that in the vast majority of cases—83 percent to be exact—the birth of that baby created a crisis situation.** By "crisis" LeMasters means that a great change occurred in the husband-wife relationship because their former behavior patterns were either inadequate or inappropriate to cope with their new role as parents. These crises occurred with equal frequency among those marriages rated as "good" and those described as "bad," indicating that the quality of the husband-wife relationship had nothing to do with a couple's initial inability to adjust to the new baby. LeMasters also explains that the parents' previous desire to have children or to remain childless neither lessened nor magnified the crisis. Furthermore, inadequate personality integration was not a factor since

* Ibid.
** E. E. LeMasters, "Parenthood as Crises," *Marriages and Family Living*, vol. 19, no. 4, Nov. 1957, pp. 352-353.

the subjects of this study were described as being personally well-adjusted.

Among the conditions LeMasters discovered contributing to stress on the new parents' own relationship were the following:

WIVES

- Loss of sleep during the first months.
- Extensive confinement to the house.
- Chronic tiredness and exhaustion.
- Curtailment of social activities.
- Giving up certain personal satisfactions.
- Loss of income from employment.
- Additional washing and ironing.
- Guilt feelings for not being a better mother.
- Concern over appearance (fear that the period of pregnancy would permanently affect their figures).

HUSBANDS

- Decline in sexual response of wife.
- Economic pressures resulting from the loss of wife's income and the additional expense of the baby.
- Interference with social life.
- Worry about a secondary pregnancy in the near future.
- A general disenchantment with the parental role.

LeMasters believes that these conditions, either singly or in combination, may precipitate a family adjustment crisis.

Many young couples may experience a certain amount

of anxiety when their first baby is born because they are suddenly faced with responsibilities that they may be emotionally or financially ill equipped to cope with. In addition they may have trouble making the transition from living as a pair to living as a trio. LeMasters explains that a father may feel "semi-isolated" because his wife must give first priority to the infant and spend less time in gratifying her husband's needs. Furthermore the physical strain of caring for the child may diminish her ability to perform as a sex partner reducing the quality and enjoyment of the relationship they shared when they were childless. Then there are those wives who feel emotionally abandoned because their husbands invest a great deal of love and attention in the child. Some young mothers become overly concerned about their appearance, misinterpreting their husbands' decreased attention as a hint that they are no longer youthful or attractive.

Perhaps the chief reason couples have problems adjusting to the birth of their first child, says LeMasters, is that parenthood has been so romanticized by our culture that its negative aspects tend to catch new parents completely by surprise. The overglorification of the maternal role often makes young women think motherhood is a state of total relaxed bliss. The crying and interrupted nights come as a nasty shock. Men, too, are often surprised that being a father amounts to a lot more than Sunday strolls in the park. This lack of preparation stems in part from an educational system which neglects to treat so important a subject as parenthood with honesty and frankness. Our schools provide career counseling and college guidance, but nowhere do we have an objective and realistic program that equates parenthood with the words "Sacrifice," "Responsibility," and "Dedication." We talk today about relevancy in education. What could be more relevant than instructing young people in the true pluses and minuses of parenthood, thereby giving them the chance to objectively decide if they want to spend a good portion of their adult lives as parents or if they would rather choose alternative life-styles?

LeMasters closes his article by saying that eventually most of the couples *did* adjust to their role as parents, but this does not necessarily mean they were happy or satisfied doing so. Adjustment, whether to parenthood or any other situation, only means an acceptance of what is, a personal adaptation to the unalterable conditions of one's life. Since being a parent is something that people can do very little about, they just have to make the best of it. Now, no one in his right mind would argue that all couples with children *only* adjust to their role as parents and find little happiness and fulfillment. Many husbands and wives enjoy raising children and do a good job of it. However, there are many whose enthusiasm for parenthood was only surface deep and with a little questioning will admit that they preferred prenatal marriage to postnatal. In fact, some new research evidence indicates that *most* couples actually experienced a higher level of marital satisfaction *before* they had children and, perhaps even more significant, childless couples were found to have a greater level of marital satisfaction than those with children.

Dr. Harold Feldman, a professor in the Department of Human Development and Family Studies at Cornell University, conducted an extensive study of 852 middle- and upper-class urban couples. He found that "those with children had a significantly lower level of marital satisfaction than did those without children." In a later study Dr. Feldman confirmed the hypothesis: "When a couple become parents the marital satisfaction declines."*

Dr. Feldman's findings were reconfirmed in a follow-up study of 268 husbands and 268 wives. Feldman reports:

Approximately 43 percent of both sexes decreased in satisfaction, about 39 percent remained the same, and approximately 18 percent increased in satisfaction, showing a statistically significant overall decrease in marital satisfaction with the birth of the first child for both sexes. It is indicated that, in general, the coming of the first child tends to be related to a decrease in marital satisfaction. Since it is unlikely that a decrease in marital satisfaction yields a baby, the cause and effect relationship is more probably in the opposite direction, i.e., having a baby causes a decrease in marital satisfaction.**

The reasons for the decline in marital satisfaction are largely the same as those which caused the initial adjustment crises following the birth of their first child. We can assume then that the psychologically, physically, and socially unsatisfactory conditions of early parenthood did

* Harold Feldman, "Changes in Marriage and Parenthood: A Methodological Design." Unpublished study.
** Harold Feldman and Michael Rogoff, "Correlates of Changes in Marital Satisfaction with the Birth of the First Child." Unpublished study.

not disappear as adjustment took place but rather that they endured and became an integral part of the family relationship. Their transformance from crises conditions occurred as the couple learned to accept the new regime as part of their daily lives. For many men and women parenthood seems to be a matter of "I'm not crazy about it but, for better or worse, I have to live with it."

Dr. Feldman and his co-researcher, Joseph H. Meyrowitz, turned up an interesting statistical finding that might in part account for the stated difference in marital satisfaction between those couples with children and those without:

> The possibility that children in the home are not affectors of marital relationships but the symptoms of different kinds of married persons is possible and the more highly romanticized values of those with children may be a cue to these differences. One finding that was significant at the .10 level relates to this conclusion. The childless couples have a higher level of the striving achievement values, intellectual stimulation and developing their personal interests. The accomplishment of these values may be perceived as being interfered with by children.*

Romantics, with their idealized notions about the way things *should* be, are often prone to disillusionment when their hopes are shot down by reality. And the high-flying idealization of motherhood and fatherhood arising from

* Harold Feldman and Joseph H. Meyrowitz, "Development of the Husband-Wife Relationship: A Research Report, Cornell University, Department of Child Development and Family Relationships, August 31, 1964, p. 153.

the culturally conditioned idea that children create a marital paradise often results in a state of disillusionment that causes an overall decline in marital satisfaction. On the other hand, those couples who have few illusions about childbearing are better prepared to accept the true satisfactions and dissatisfactions of parenthood. And those husbands and wives who decide to raise a family with absolutely no preconceived belief that children will improve their marriages will probably be the best emotionally equipped parents of all.

What seems to be the real issue here is that most people unquestioningly accept the Myth of Family Instincts without examining their own personal attitudes toward parenthood. The result is that many couples experience a persistent feeling of dissatisfaction that they are loath to trace to their children. In their article, "A Longitudinal Study in Marital Satisfaction," Paris L. Bethel and Eleanore B. Luckey say:

> . . . the actual presence or number of children in the family is probably not so important in marital happiness as are the attitudes of the couples regarding children.*

If this is true, as we suspect it is, our earlier proposition about realistic family education for high school and college students would be invaluable in helping them to discover what they really want out of their marriages and their lives. And this in the long run will produce happier

---

* Paris L. Bethel and Eleanore B. Luckey, "A Longitudinal Study in Marital Satisfaction," *Sociology and Social Research*, 1966 (Vol. 50, no. 2), p. 217.

and more stable marriages because couples who truly desire children will have them knowing what parenthood actually entails while those who desire to remain childless will not become parents simply because of cultural pressure.

There is a trend, though by no means a landslide, among young educated couples to either remain childless or to postpone childbearing for an indefinite period of time. These are the so-called "make love, not babies" marriages in which both husband and wife feel that childbearing would interfere with their careers, education, or other goals. This attitude can be traced to two sources. The first is that higher education is making more and more young men and women aware of the many alternatives available for personal fulfillment outside of traditional family life. For many of these couples the suburban home, the two cars, and the 2.3 children are a moribund dream of another generation; a static and sterile way of life that restricts individual development and expression by promoting security over freedom. The second source is the flowering of women's liberation that not only makes women aware of their options but provides them with the psychological strength to take them. For the first time women are realizing that they are not isolated freaks for wanting to step outside of the restricted sphere that their mothers, grandmothers, and great-grandmothers accepted as their "proper place."

VI

Alternatives
to Motherhood

The purpose of this chapter is to show women that motherhood is not the only path to personal fulfillment and to expose the falsehoods, the half-truths and psychosocial pressures that have for so long excluded women from the career community. We do not propose to list all the alternatives to motherhood; the Federal government has already done this in the *Dictionary of Occupational Titles*, a publication of the United States Employment Service which contains the definitions of the 21,643 occupations open to men *and* women in our economy. The dictionary describes each of these jobs and sets forth the minimum qualifications necessary for filling them. No matter what the requirements of a specific job might be, Title VII of the 1964 Civil Rights Act forbids discrimination on the basis of sex and a qualified female who applies for a job, whether white collar or blue collar, skilled or unskilled, professional or nonprofessional, cannot be excluded from that job simply because she is a woman. The law clearly states that the burden of proof of the unsuitability of a job for a woman is on the *employer*, and even if one woman is judged unsuited for a particular occupation, this is not an across-the-board closing of that occupation to all women. This means that *legally* women have the same career alternatives as men.

In practice, however, things are very different and we intend here to examine some of the obstacles that keep women from objectively considering a break with the traditional wife-mother role.

Before we do this, we should point out that there are two types of alternatives to motherhood. The first is having no children at all and actively pursuing a career or profession. The second is combining a career with motherhood, which is a modification of the traditional mother role. Of the four major obstacles to female alternatives, the first three apply to both categories, while the fourth, the Myth of the Working Mother, deals specifically with the problems and questions that women may have in deciding on a dual role. Let us begin by discussing the first barrier to objective consideration of the alternatives to motherhood; male prejudice.

The Male Attitude

In her book, *Up From the Pedestal: Selected Writings in the History of American Feminism*, Aileen S. Kraditor includes an essay by Thomas R. Dew entitled "Dissertation on the Characteristic Differences Between the Sexes," which, although written over one hundred years ago, contains the identical prejudices that men today have toward women. Mr. Dew tells us:

The relative position of the sexes in the social and political world, may certainly be looked upon as the result of organization. The greater physical strength of the man enables him to occupy the foreground in the picture. He leaves the domestic scenes; he plunges into the turmoil and bustle of an active, selfish world; in his journey through life he has to encounter innumerable difficulties, hardships and labors which constantly beset him. His mind must be nerved against them. Hence courage and boldness are his attributes. It is his province, undismayed, to stand against the rude shocks of the world; to meet with a lion's heart the dangers which threaten him. He is the shield of woman, destined by nature to guard and protect her. Her inferior strength and sedentary habits confine her within the domestic circle; she is kept aloof from the bustle and storm of active life, she is not familiarized to the out-of-doors dangers and hardships of a cold and scuffling world: timidity and modesty are her attributes. In the great strife which is constantly forward around her, there are powers engaged which her inferior physical strength prevents her from encountering. She must rely upon the strength of others; man must be engaged in her cause. . . . Grace, modesty and loveliness are the charms which constitute her power. By these, she creates the magic spell that subdues to her will the more mighty physical powers by which she is surrounded. Her attributes are rather of a passive than active character. Her power is more emblematical of that divinity: it subdues without an effort and almost creates by mere volition; whilst man must wind his way through the difficult and intricate mazes of philosophy; with pain and toil, tracing effects to their causes, and unraveling the deep mysteries of nature— storing his mind with useful knowledge, and exercising, training and perfecting his intellectual powers, whilst he cultivates his strength and hardens and matures his courage; all with a view of enabling him to assert his rights, and exercise a greater sway over those around him. Woman we behold dependent and weak; but out of that very weakness and dependence springs an irresistible power. She may pursue her studies too— not however with a view of triumphing in the senate chamber—not with a view of leading armies into combat, or of enabling her to bring into more formidable action the physical power which nature has conferred on her.*

Thomas R. Dew, his eloquence notwithstanding, could not be further from the truth by asserting that women are physically, intellectually, and emotionally weaker than men. Before we proceed to show why, we should mention the fact that Thomas R. Dew was a proslavery pamphleteer who wrote at great length about the "natural" inferiority of the black race and of the correctness of white domination. It is evident from Mr. Dew's writing that he held the same lord-and-master attitude toward women as he did toward blacks.

And we do not doubt for one moment that this same lord-and-master attitude influences the thinking of the majority of men today and contributes to their inability and unwillingness to treat women as equals.

* Thomas R. Dew, "Dissertation on the Characteristic Differences Between the Sexes," *Up From the Pedestal*, Aileen S. Kraditor, ed. (Quadrangle Books, Inc., Chicago, 1968), pp. 45-46.

The male supremacy argument begins with the idea that because men have greater muscle power they are physically superior to females in all respects. From this premise the argument goes on to say that because of their more powerful physique, men are better suited to cope with the harsh emotional and intellectual demands of the business world. If we examine the foundation of this argument we find it full of flaws, and, as a consequence, we also find that the superstructure that rests upon it, the male-dominated society, is very shaky indeed. The fact is that men are *not* physically superior to women. Says noted anthropologist Ashley Montagu:

Women endure all sorts of devitalizing conditions better than men: starvation, exposure, fatigue, shock, illness, and the like. This immediately raises the question of the supposed "weakness" of the female. Is not the female supposed to be the "weaker vessel"? "Weakness" is a misleading word that has, in this connection, confused most people. "Feminine weakness" has generally meant that the female is more fragile and in general less strong than the male. But the fact is that the female is *constitutionally* stronger than the male, and only muscularly less powerful; she has greater stamina and lives longer. The male pays heavily for his larger body build and muscular power. Because his expenditure of energy is greater than that of the female, he burns himself out more rapidly and hence dies at an earlier age.

Where, now, are the much-vaunted advantages of larger size and muscular power? Are they biologically fitter in any way? Are they, any longer, even socially advantageous? The answer is that whatever benefits men may have derived from larger size and muscular power in the past, they have in our own time outlived them. Today the advantages are mostly with the smaller bodied, less muscularly powerful female.*

And going beyond muscle power, we also find that women are, and have been for thousands of years, genetically and biologically superior to men in many important ways. In his book, *The Basic Facts of Human Heredity*, Amram Scheinfeld makes this indisputably clear:

> Altogether, it is now recognized that in almost every important disease—mental, organic, functional, infectious—the sex of the individual plays a role in its development and severity. And most amazing it is becoming increasingly clear that *males, not females, are the weaker sex*, biologically. For, as a group males are more often born defective, are more likely to suffer from hereditary ailments, are inherently more susceptible to most major diseases, and when afflicted are more likely to succumb. Females are inherently at a disadvantage in only a few categories—*afflictions linked with childbearing* (italics ours) and their sex organs; cancers restricted to their sex; gallstones; and diabetes, goiter and certain other glandular diseases.**

These findings have an almost revolutionary impact on the entire structure and social role assignment of modern

* Ashley Montagu, *The Natural Superiority of Women*, Revised Edition (Collier Books, New York 1968), pp. 58-59.
** Amram Scheinfeld, *The Basic Facts of Human Heredity* (Washington Square Press, Inc., New York 1961), p. 74.

culture. Until the Machine Age, men *had* to do the work because there were no technological alternatives to brute strength, but today only 10 percent of the available occupations require great muscle power while 90 percent can be done equally well by both sexes. Thus, it no longer is necessary to assign the role of provider only to men. Furthermore, on a strictly pragmatic basis, it would probably be advisable to have more women contributing to the family finances because their lower susceptibility to incapacitating illness and their greater life expectancy makes them more reliable providers than their biologically weaker husbands. The implications of this in terms of alternatives to motherhood are interesting to think about. The most obvious is the possibility that women of the future may limit their motherhood role to childbearing while their husbands stay home and take over childrearing.

For those male supremacists who cling tenaciously to the idea that there will always be a 10 percent occupational advantage in their favor because of their muscular superiority, we have a bit of bad news. That edge may be substantially reduced. We asked New York gynecologist Dr. Richard M. Hausknecht about his thoughts on male-female physical differences and if women could conceivably handle the really "he-man" occupations that require massive strength. For example, "Could there ever be a female Joe Namath?" To this, Dr. Hausknecht replied:

> I don't know why we're not going to have a female Joe Namath. There are some women whose bodies can be trained to develop muscularly in such a way as to

permit them to do the things that males normally do. . . . from earliest days of life, the female body is not subjected to the same kind of training as a male's, so that by the time a woman becomes mature her muscles can't do what a man's muscles can do. But I think if both male and female children were to be reared identically, the differences would not be that great. Now of course the bone structure of the female is different from the bone structure of the male, it's lighter. But to date nobody has really tried to get around this problem."

And when asked if we could look forward to the day when there would be female construction workers and auto mechanics, Dr. Hausknecth said emphatically:

Oh, yes! Absolutely! Again it's a matter of where you start. If you're going to start with a mature woman, clearly not. But if you're going to start from the cradle training males and females equally in terms of their physical skills, then I can see no reason why females can't be plumbers and carpenters and all the other things that men are. I'm just not convinced there's a genetic or endocrinologic excuse for many of the things that we think separate males and females. I think they are sociologic. They're part of our society. . . . if you change the structure of society you will also change many of the things we think are immutable. I think the male-female division of labor is basically a false one, and I have thought so for many years.

The male predilection for associating bigness with superiority has led many men to believe that because they are generally larger than women that they also have an advantage in intelligence, especially since it has been known for some time that males, on the average, have bigger brains than women. To set the record straight, brain size has little if anything to do with intellectual capabilities. Elephants have bigger brains than humans, Cro-Magnon man, a race of prehistoric cave dwellers, had a brain cavity 14½ percent larger than modern man, and the largest brain on record was possessed by an idiot. What *does* have a relation to intelligence is the number of convolutions of the brain, and scientists have found some very convoluted small brains and some relatively smooth large ones.

Intelligence itself is a rather vague concept and there are almost as many definitions of it as there are psychologists and other behavioral scientists who try to define it. However, what we have measured of intelligence through the various I.Q. tests and tests of general mental ability has registered insignificant differences between the sexes, and if we compare the nature of these differences, *females* come out a little better than males. Blair, Jones, and Simpson, the authors of *Educational Psychology*, report:

> In general, studies of school achievement agree that girls make consistently better scores than boys. . . . Girls are less apt to be retarded readers and spellers and they are less apt to suffer such speech incoordinations as stammering and stuttering. . . . Although on the average girls excel in general school achievement . . . boys seem to have a slight edge in arithmetic, history, geography, and science. Such differences as do exist

seem to parallel so closely what we know about the interests of each sex that it is safe to conclude that a great part of these differences are products of the roles which are set for children and not due to innate factors. A school environment which favors either sex is likely to produce superiority in achievement for that sex.*

There is a definite relationship here to what Dr. Hausknecth said concerning the socio-cultural influences in the physical development of males and females. Just as we actively condition boys to use and develop their muscles, we also condition them to be receptive to mathematics, mechanics, and the sciences. Ours is an economy based on technology and science which we believe are appropriate vocational areas for males and not for females. Thus boys are taught to tune in to biology, physics, statistics, and mathematics in order to prepare themselves for the complexities of the business world. By the time they have completed their schooling they have a definite advantage in marketable skills, while female college graduates are often forced to take secretarial courses in order to get jobs. In no way does this mean that women do not have the intellectual abilities to deal with the problems of business, it is just that a male-dominated society has seen fit to exclude them from careers as engineers, architects, accountants, and doctors by killing their initial motivation to learn the basic skills necessary for these jobs. If we provided girls with the same motivational pattern as boys they would probably

* G. M. Blair, R. S. Jones, and R. H. Simpson, *Educational Psychology*, Second Edition (The Macmillan Company, New York 1962), p. 150.

do just as well in these fields. And, if their overall learning ability is any clue, they may even do a little better.

Perhaps the greatest psychological damage resulting from this masculine belief in feminine intellectual inequality is the fact that women, regardless of their aptitudes and abilities, are all lumped into one vocational classification: housewife and mother. Sociologist Theodore Caplow comments on this:

> This occupation is the only one which shows approximately the same distribution of intelligence and of all aptitudes as the general population. One of the reasons for the widespread maladjustment of housewives may be inferred from the circumstances that the same job requirements are imposed on morons and on women of superior intelligence. And there is no age requirement either. Girls of ten and upward may be able to keep house competently.*

The United States Department of Labor, through its publication *The Dictionary of Occupational Titles*, lends some validity to Caplow's statement. Although the dictionary does not list "mother" or "housewife" as occupational classifications, it does come close with the job title "mother's helper." The duties of this job are listed as cooking, cleaning, changing beds and linens, washing, ironing, watching children and keeping them out of mischief. The dictionary goes on to say that no special training is required for the job of mother's helper and that it can be done by a young person.

* Theodore Caplow, *The Sociology of Work* (McGraw-Hill Book Company, New York 1964), pp. 260-261.

Of course no one would say that there are no special talents over and above those required for being a mother's helper involved in being a competent mother. A good mother must have the intelligence and sensitivity to be able to promote the psychological, social, and intellectual development of her child. However, a good deal of a mother's daily activities undeniably involve the tasks listed above and these cannot help but color her feeling of accomplishment and personal satisfaction. The question now is, "Where does this leave the educated and aware woman who finds little challenge and joy in the repetitive tasks of the traditional wife-mother role?" In the past the answer was *Kinder, Kuchen, und Kirche* (children, kitchen, and church) because male supremacy was at its height and these were the alternatives (if you can call them that) that husbands provided for their wives. But today the picture has changed somewhat, and educated women are becoming increasingly aware of their abilities to function in other areas. The Census Bureau tells us that the more educated a woman is the less likely she is to have children, or at least a lot of them.

The bureau provides these statistics concerning a woman's education and the number of children she has:

Completed level of education	Average number of children
No education	4.9
Grade school	3.04
High school	2.03
College	1.83

As far as our discussion of the alternatives to motherhood is concerned, there are several assumptions that may be drawn from these figures. The first is that with a higher level of education comes a greater awareness of what a woman is and is not capable of doing. The second is that the more educated a woman becomes the less likely she is to turn to childbearing in order to find fulfillment. The third is that once educated, a woman has the same desire as man to use her knowledge and skills and therefore does not fill her life with lots of children who would keep her from doing this. And perhaps this is what men have been afraid of all the time. By indoctrinating women with the idea that they are intellectually inferior and by denying them access to higher education, as has historically been the case, they kept women from realizing their intellectual capabilities and thereby reserved for themselves the top positions in the social order. But as women begin to use their I.Q.'s, the myth of male intellectual supremacy weakens and men, so long the rulers, will be forced to share their positions with the ladies. In the not-too-distant future women will be fully aware of the fact that not only do they have the capacity for baby talk, but also for communicating effectively and intelligently over the conference table. This awareness will go a long way toward providing innumerable alternatives to motherhood.

Although some males can be convinced that women may be intellectually and physically their equals, they will draw the line when it comes to emotions. "It's been a fact of experience," said one corporation executive, "that women, no matter how much they have on the ball, just can't handle the stresses of business. Women aren't built to take the psychological pressures . . . they become overly emotional." To this, Ashley Montagu says:

Women don't fight, don't curse, don't lose their tempers as often as men do; they seldom get drunk and exceedingly rarely commit acts of violence against other persons. Though quicker on the uptake, they do not jump to conclusions as hastily and as unconsiderably as men. Women tend to avoid the trigger responses of the male; as a result, they do not go off half-cocked as frequently as the male does. Women tend to keep their emotional balance better than men do. In short, women use their emotions a great deal more efficiently than men, and not in the "emotional" manner that men imply when they use the word disparagingly in connection with women. In this sense women are positively *less* emotional than men. In the accurate sense of the word, women are more emotional and have their emotions more effectively under control than do men.*

Men and women have the same emotions, the difference rests in the way they handle them. Men internalize their emotions because they have been socially conditioned to believe it is unmanly to cry when things go wrong or to show elation when things go right. Women on the other hand are not socially proscribed from expressing the full range of their emotions. They easily get their feelings out in the open and therefore are able to handle them in a more healthy way. The psychological benefits of female "emotionality" actually make women emotionally stronger than men. Says psychology professor James C. Coleman, "Males outnumber females among

* *The Natural Superiority of Women*, pp. 89-90.

first admissions to mental hospitals in about the ratio of 4 to 3."* Men also suffer from such psychosomatic ailments as ulcers at a much higher rate than women. And accident proneness, a psychological predisposition to accidents stemming from an inability to cope with stress or from latent personality disturbances, is more than twice as prevalent among men as women. And Dr. Louis I. Dublin, author of *The Facts of Life from Birth to Death* says:

> Men are more likely to kill themselves than are women. In the United States, male suicides have usually outnumbered female suicides by slightly more than three to one.**

It would appear then that the stereotype of the "emotional" female exists more in male mythology than in fact. Women *are* in better control of their emotions, and because they also tend to get over emotional crises more quickly than men, probably have greater psychological staying power in high stress situations such as business. Says Dr. John J. Pietrofesa, Assistant Professor of Guidance and Counseling at Wayne University:

> The education and guidance of women today should stress the noncompetitive and complementary roles men and women play in regard to each other. Women should not be taught to assume masculine characteristics

* James C. Coleman, *Abnormal Psychology and Modern Life*, Third Edition (Scott, Foresman and Company, Chicago 1964), p. 268.
** Louis I. Dublin, *The Facts of Life from Birth to Death* (Macmillan Company, New York 1951), p. 260.

of personality and emotional adjustment on the justification that these are superior modes of behavior. A good case can be made for just the opposite position.*

Although men have believed that females are the inferior sex, the height of male arrogance is yet to be revealed. For a long time males have excluded females from the business world by saying that women do not desire status, position, and advancement. They claim that the competitive urge is strictly masculine in nature, while the need to be protected and pampered represents true femininity, a position many men now support to defend their own positions. In his article, "Difference in Perception of Desired Job Characteristics of the Same and the Opposite Sex," Ronald J. Burke says:

> The current influx of females into the traditionally male endeavors is probably heightening the pressures for success that males experience. The threat posed by females in academic and professional occupations is a real one. This increased threat can be minimized, according to the defensive comparison principle if females are seen as incapable of wanting the same things as males. This would account for the male stereotype of opposite sex preferences. . . .**

On all accounts, the male stereotype of the female has produced a very shabby case for masculine supremacy,

---

* John J. Pietrofesa, "Women and the World of Work," *Catholic Education Review* (April, 1964), p. 259.
** Ronald J. Burke, "Differences in Perception of Desired Job Characteristics of the Same and the Opposite Sex," *Journal of Genetic Psychology* (1966, 106 [1]), pp. 44-45.

but the strange thing is that women have believed it. And the result of thousands of years of indoctrination by a male dominated society has been the *female attitude*, the next obstacle in seeking alternatives to motherhood.

The Female Attitude

The female attitude, as it pertains to alternatives to motherhood, has two components: *The Female Occupational Inferiority Complex* and the *False Concept of Femininity*; both of which are direct derivatives of male prejudice. Let's begin by examining the first.

Women have been conditioned to believe that they lack the capabilities of men to find success and fulfillment outside the home. Psychiatrist Dr. Lionel Ovesey explains how and why this occurs:

> The social order is so arranged that status accrues to men solely by virtue of the fact that they are men. The polarities of masculinity and femininity are identified respectively with positive and negative value judgments. Masculinity represents strength, dominance, superiority; femininity represents weakness, submissiveness, inferiority. The former is equated with success; the latter with failure. It is true that these values are cultural stereotypes that express primarily the historical prejudices of the men in the culture. However, it would be safe to say that men and women alike make use of them in appraising each other's behavior.
>
> The adaptational responses of women to these institutional pressures in many ways are similar to the responses of members of the minority group in a caste system. Many women—although by no means all—

consciously reject this prejudicial picture of themselves, but it is doubtful that few if any completely escape its deleterious effects on an unconscious level. Women must struggle against deflation of the self-esteem and the self-contempt that goes with it.*

If Dr. Ovesey is correct in his analysis, it is not difficult to see why many women cannot assume roles other than that of the traditional wife-mother. A male dominated society has established the psycho-social criteria for success, declared by fiat that only men can meet these criteria while at the same time telling females that their "feminine" traits, largely the product of false male stereotyping, are thoroughly inadequate in the competitive career world. Internalizing these male notions and making them a part of their attitude toward themselves, women become convinced that they lack the capabilities of males and attempt to combat their feelings of low self-esteem by denying career aspirations and creating for themselves an environment in which they feel they can function effectively and achieve a modicum of status and self-worth. In this environment—the home—they swell with pride over each successful soufflé, thrive on compliments telling them that their houses are spotless, and, most of all, approach euphoria as friends and relatives pay endless tribute to the wonderful job they are doing in bringing up their children. "This," they say to themselves, "is all that a woman can hope for, or should hope for."

* Lionel Ovesey, "Masculine Aspirations in Women," *Psychiatry* (November, 1956), p. 341.

The Female Occupational Inferiority Complex is most evident in the attitudes that women have toward work and in their reasons for choosing particular jobs. If you question men about their career objectives, aside from making a good living, they will tell you about their desires for advancement, to put their educations to use, to make names for themselves, or realize some important personal goals. These are *primary* work motives. But women for the most part will respond to the same question by offering *secondary* motivations which reflect the female attitude that their primary fulfillment will not come through their work but through their activities as housewife and mother. Women view careers as temporary ways of supporting themselves until they find husbands; as necessary evils to help their husbands through college or professional school; as a good way to keep busy until they become pregnant. Men see the office as a place to meet challenges while women see it as a place to meet men. And even professional women, teachers for example, see their career training and experience as a kind of insurance, something to fall back on in the event that their husbands suffer business reverses or become ill and unable to earn a living.

Women also tend to gravitate toward those jobs which have the easiest entrance requirements and which require the shortest training periods. Men become doctors, dentists, and lawyers; women become medical technicians, dental assistants, and legal secretaries. Men go on for advanced degrees and become college professors; women take undergraduate education courses and become grade school teachers. (Incidentally, contrary to popular belief,

167

there are *fewer* women today who have the advanced degrees of master of arts or doctor of philosophy than there were back in the 1920s and 1930s.) The two reasons for this are that women see little value in spending all those years in training for a profession when they will only have to give up their jobs in order to bear and rear children. And second, many women honestly believe that they are unable to compete with men and therefore aim for lower level jobs which they feel they are capable of handling. This lack of self-confidence is a mammoth barrier to even thinking about alternatives to motherhood. Janice LaRoche, founder and director of the Career Workshop for Women in New York City has recognized this occupational inferiority complex and uses group therapy to overcome it. Mrs. LaRoche explains it this way:

> Certainly many men think that women can't handle high level jobs, and in some ways they're right because women are not trained or prepared for them. Women don't have the same kind of scope for employment as men. They lack the initiative to handle problems out of their own resources. They are trained to follow instructions. Women frequently confer with men in order to be told what to do as opposed to men who confer with each other to get opinions out of which they will make their own decisions. Men see themselves as decision makers, women do not.
>
> We (the Career Workshop for Women) try to develop an awareness in women of how limited their functioning has been. We show them that where they

think they've been taking initiative, they're really taking it within the scope defined by men. For example, the boss says be my secretary or be my office manager and take all the initiative you want. You know, type a letter in the best way you know how. He defines the limits. She's not thinking in terms of how to improve the office or how to bring in more business. She's not thinking in the same kind of terms of initiative expansion as a man is. Nor is she thinking that if she develops a skill that she's going to get his job when he moves up. The most she can hope for is to become the secretary to the boss. That's the high spot.

Most women have to become aware of how limited their functioning is, then we can begin to compensate for the lack of scope they've had in their upbringing. Women . . . simply lack the experience. They miss opportunities because they simply don't know what's going on, what the business structure is. They don't know what the aim of the business is or what people are doing. This may come from their cultural preparation. Boys have a certain worldliness from communicating with other boys. . . . in the college dorm while the boys are talking about computers, science, or business, women are talking about dates, clothes and hairdo's. They aren't getting the scope because they just don't know what these subjects are about.

Women don't have the opportunity to test and measure themselves in the work world. One of the reasons that I established the Career Workshop is that women don't have this period of testing themselves at work, and they flounder when they go back to work.

They don't understand why they are so inadequate and we have to help them understand why they are so inadequate and we have to help them understand the reasons for their inadequacies so that they don't take it personally and think they're stupid, when in reality they just missed out on experience.

One of the nice things about the workshop is that we have mixed-age levels and younger women see the problems that older women have in respect to personal growth, productivity, and career. . . . I've had many young women of 23 or 24 who jump out of the workshop and back into college. Some go back and get their masters or Ph.D.'s because from listening to the experience of the older women they realize that they had better have the preparation for a career so that they won't get into the same bind that the older women did. The only way for a woman to beat the system as it stands now is to have lots of plans. Only by being aware of the problems and planning everything out is a woman going to make it.

But even if women do realize that they are capable of functioning in business, and even if they do psychologically commit themselves to finding alternative life-styles to motherhood, society places many barriers before them. Male prejudice, which we have already discussed is one, and active job discrimination which we will talk about later is another. These are obvious and can be fought out in the open. However, there are subtle barriers that reinforce a woman's belief in her inability to choose freely from the range of occupations that are legally open to her. For example, when high school or college students go for career counseling they are often given a battery of tests which attempt to identify their vocational aptitudes and interests in order to help them choose a career. One of the most frequently used tests is the *Strong Vocational Blank*, which has two forms; one for men and one for women. The *Strong Vocational Blank for Men* covers a broad range of careers and has many more test items than the form for women which contains fewer items and thus a narrower choice of careers. Kirk E. Farnsworth investigated this problem and presented his finding in an article entitled, "Vocational Interests of Women." Dr. Farnsworth reports:

> The vocational interests of women are indeed complex, not to be explained away by the reductionist dichotomy of "career versus home." In other words, the high specificity of structure—many identifiable factors—strongly suggests that women's vocational interests are far more complex than has widely been assumed.
>
> The results of any analysis, however, are highly dependent upon the restrictions of the data to be analyzed. One restriction is that the dimensions of women's vocational interests are partially a function of the conception of those interests by those who construct the instrument to be used, in this case, the SVIB (*Strong Vocational Interest Blank for Women*).*

In a very specific way, Dr. Farnsworth's comments on the SVIB underline the fact that everyone but women

* Kirk E. Farnsworth, "Vocational Interests of Women," *Journal of Applied Psychology* (October, 1969), p. 357.

has a hand in defining their "proper" vocational interests. Of course most women would take issue with this and say that they chose to become mothers. But is this really so? As Mrs. LaRoche has pointed out, women make their decisions within the bounds set by a male-dominated society. If we recognize the existence of a Female Occupational Inferiority Complex, then we must also recognize the possibility that childbearing may be a reaction against its psychologically damaging effects. When certain women become mothers they do so with the hope that childbearing will give them the feelings of usefulness, accomplishment, and prestige they believe they are incapable of finding outside the home.

Some women believe that their employability is limited by the fact they would sacrifice their femininity if they took a job in any of the traditionally male fields. In fact, many are convinced that women who pursue careers *instead* of becoming wives and mothers are not only unfeminine, but psychologically abnormal as well. This concept of femininity, or more accurately, *false concept of femininity* rests on our cultural tendency to confer sexual identity on a person according to the occupation that he or she follows. Amram Scheinfeld made a detailed study of sexual identification by occupation and summarized his findings in the chart on the next page.*

What Scheinfeld shows graphically is that society shuts women out of many occupations by labeling them unfeminine. But is there anything about a certain job that

* (Used by permission from: Amram Scheinfeld, *The New You and Heredity*, p. 452.)

"MASCULINITY" AND "FEMININITY"

(How various classifications of men and women rank
according to average scores in the "M-F" tests)

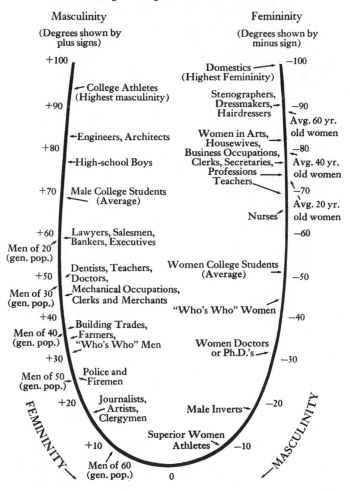

Masculinity — (Degrees shown by plus signs)

Femininity — (Degrees shown by minus sign)

+100

+90 — College Athletes (Highest masculinity)

+80 — Engineers, Architects / High-school Boys

+70 — Male College Students (Average)

+60 — Lawyers, Salesmen, Bankers, Executives — Men of 20 (gen. pop.)

+50 — Dentists, Teachers, Doctors, — Men of 30 (gen. pop.) — Mechanical Occupations, Clerks and Merchants

+40 — Building Trades, Farmers, "Who's Who" Men — Men of 40 (gen. pop.)

+30 — Police and Firemen — Men of 50 (gen. pop.)

+20 — Journalists, Artists, Clergymen

+10 — Men of 60 (gen. pop.)

0

Domestics (Highest Femininity) — −100

Stenographers, Dressmakers, Hairdressers — −90 — Avg. 60 yr. old women

Women in Arts, Housewives, Business Occupations, Clerks, Secretaries, Professions Teachers — −80 — Avg. 40 yr. old women

Nurses — −70 — Avg. 20 yr. old women

−60

Women College Students (Average) — −50

"Who's Who" Women — −40

Women Doctors or Ph.D.'s — −30

Male Inverts — −20

Superior Women Athletes — −10

FEMININITY   MASCULINITY

(Adapted from: Amram Scheinfeld, The New You and Heredity, p. 452.) Used by permission.

173

truly affects a woman's ability to be a woman? The answer is no. It is only society's opinion of women that influences their concept of femininity because there is nothing innately masculine or feminine about any job. Says Lawrence K. Frank:

> How each culture defines . . . the masculine and feminine roles gives the individual the initial orientation toward the other sex. . . . Maleness and femaleness are biological, but masculinity and femininity are cultural. . . . The prescribed masculine and feminine roles may not be congenial or feasible to everyone despite their male or female genitals. . . . What looks like an organic, biological event . . . is a very complicated psycho-cultural performance, to understand which we should know, what cultural traditions have patterned the individual's image of himself, and evaluation of his or her conception of the masculine or feminine roles, his or her evaluation and expectation of sex and its place and functioning in human life.*

Relating this to motherhood, we can say that women have the ability to become mothers; that is part of their *femaleness*. But the desire to have children is part of their *femininity*, and that is endowed by the culture. The reason we say that the cultural concept of femininity is false is because women never really had a hand in deciding what is or is not feminine. Ashley Montagu points out

* Lawrence K. Frank, "The Psychocultural Approach in Sex Research," in *Sexual Behavior in American Society*, edited by Jerome Himelhoch and Sylvia F. Fava (W. W. Norton & Co., Inc., New York 1955), pp. 6-7.

174

that, "The behavior of women in our culture has largely been conditioned by and in response to the behavior of males toward them.* Men have said that it is unfeminine for women to compete with them in business, so women feel obliged to choose occupations that are both non-competitive and subservient, and they do this in the belief that it is "feminine" for them to work at such jobs. And since men have always valued fertility in women and considered childbearing as their greatest accomplishment, women, regardless of their own wishes, have felt that they had to have children or sacrifice their femininity. Thus in many cases it is neither femaleness nor femininity that arouses the desire to have children, but rather the desire of certain women to be *thought* of as feminine.

A contributing factor to the false concept of femininity is the notion that a woman is abnormal if she does not want the things that women "should" want; specifically, a home, a husband, and children. However, research evidence shows that women who do not have or want these things are *not* the maladjusted, bitter, and resentful old maids that we have pictured. In his study, "The Personal and Social Adjustment of the Never-Married Woman," Dr. Luther G. Baker compares the psychological adjustment of 38 married mothers with that of 38 never-married women. The instrument that Dr. Baker used in his study was the *California Test of Personality, 1953 Revision.* When the results of the tests were graphed, they looked like the chart on the following page.

* *The Natural Superiority of Women*, p. 50.

COMPARISON OF PERCENTILE RANKS OF MARRIED
AND NEVER-MARRIED WOMEN

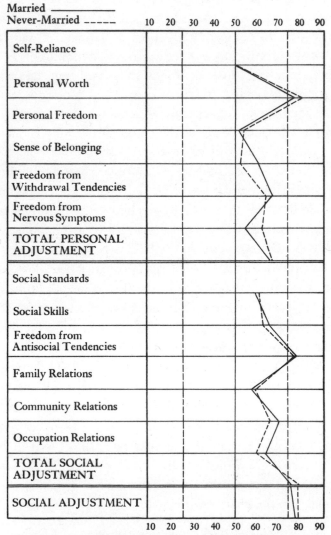

(Source: Luther G. Baker, Jr. "The Personal and Social Adjustment of
Never-Married Women," Journal of Marriage and the Family, August
1966, p. 475.) Used by permission.

In analyzing his data, Baker states:

As measured by this test, there is no support for the assumption that adequate personal and social adjustment is possible to women only if they marry and bear children. Not only do the never-married women in this study achieve, on the whole, higher-than-average scores, they score as well on every item as the control group of married mothers.*

Dr. Baker goes on to present some assumptions which may be helpful to women weighing the pros and cons of choosing alternatives to motherhood:

Popular opinion notwithstanding, this study demonstrates that personal fulfillment, insofar as it can be realistically measured, does not depend on marriage and parenthood. The never-married subjects in this investigation expressed no feelings of frustration, no sense of not being a "whole person" as a consequence of being unmarried. Their sense of personal worth comes not from their biological functions as a female but from their social function as a human being, from what they perceive as a creative contribution to their significant society. Just as insemination is what a man does with his biology, so fetal development is what women do with their biology. It is obviously true that the physiological involvement is considerably greater for a woman than for a man, but it remains nonetheless a function of the body and not of the "self." Fulfill-

* Luther G. Baker, Jr., "The Personal and Social Adjustment of Never-Married Women," *Journal of Marriage and the Family* (August, 1968), p. 475.

ment as a mother comes not from giving birth to a child (not all women who bear children are "fulfilled"), but from the subsequent contribution she makes to the developmental needs of that child. Furthermore, just as a man is able to make a creative contribution to some significant society and . . . achieve a high sense of personal worth without ever impregnating a woman, so a woman can accomplish a similar sense of personal fulfillment without ever having been impregnated by a man.*

Fortunately for men, their contributions to their various significant societies—professions, corporations, and academic communities—are evaluated solely in terms of their intrinsic value and do not in any way involve the masculinity of the man who is making the contribution. Unfortunately, the same is not true for women. Their significant societies—friends, relatives, and neighbors—actively promote the idea that children are women's greatest contribution and definitely *do* question the femininity and psycho-sexual adjustment of those who choose to remain childless in order to pursue a career. This social attitude, as we have said, is internalized by women, and results in a conditioned maternal drive.

The final pressure that turns women away from considering alternatives to their conventional role is the fear that by adopting "masculine" career patterns they would be defeminizing themselves to the degree of eliminating their sexual desirability. Obviously this reflects the male

* Ibid., p. 478.

attitude that women should be sexual objects whose primary functions are gratifying a man's erotic needs and having his babies and that women who aspire to do other than these things are incapable of normal heterosexual relationships. However, recent years have brought more and more women out of their domestic environment and into the labor force so that today we have approximately 28 million working women who are modifying their traditional role. Has this reduced the quality of the interaction between the sexes? Dr. Nelson Foote believes that the opposite is true and that liberation of women actually improves their ability to relate to men more effectively. Says Dr. Foote:

. . . the decline of segregation of roles need not mean homogenization of roles inside the home any more than outside the home. It can indeed mean the emergence of many new forms of complementarity. When roles are highly segregated in rigid traditional compartments, interaction is limited in both amount and range. With more interaction between husband and wife—more time spent together in more situations—more kinds of interaction can develop.

Despite the professed fears of some foreign—and even some native—observers of American life, the decline of segregation of the sexes has not reduced erotic and romantic behavior; instead, interest in these, and time spent in enjoying them, both directly and vicariously, have conspicuously heightened. The repertoire of masculine and feminine sexual roles has widened among most segments of our society. Many now enjoy experiences that once were the possession or prerogative of a few.*

It appears then that there is less and less justification for the attitude that women have toward themselves and their role in society. And for women considering alternatives to motherhood, the issue presently at hand should not be whether or not they are capable of functioning in a business environment because objective evidence shows that they are; nor should they concern themselves with a loss of femininity or femaleness because there is nothing mutually exclusive about being a breadwinner and being a woman. These are paper barriers to female alternatives that can easily be torn down by a simple change in the way a woman views herself. What *should* be of concern is the real obstacle faced by working women and that is the general prejudice of most firms and companies against advancing their women employees.

Female Employment Discrimination

In spite of the laws forbidding employment discrimination, the April 1967 *Manpower Report of the President* states that "women are concentrated to a considerable extent in low-skilled, low-paid jobs" and "their representation among professional workers has actually declined (from 40 percent in 1950 to 37 percent in 1966)."** These

* Nelson N. Foote, "New Roles for Men and Women," *Journal of Marriage and the Family* (November, 1961), p. 329.
** Department of Labor, *Manpower Report of The President* (Washington, D.C.: United States Government Printing Office, 1957), p. 133.

comparative statistics show that women doing the same work as men do not receive equal pay:

MEDIAN WAGE OR SALARY INCOME OF WORKERS IN 1968

Selected major occupation group	Year-round full-time workers	
	Women	Men
Professional, technical, kindred workers	$6,691	$10,151
Managers, officials, proprietors (except farm)	5,635	10,340
Clerical, kindred workers	4,789	7,351
Sales workers	3,461	8,549
Craftsmen, foremen, kindred workers	4,625	7,978
Operatives, kindred workers	3,991	6,738
Service workers (except private household)	3,332	6,058
Private household workers	1,523	*

(Source: U.S. Department of Commerce, Bureau of Census: *Current Population Reports*, No. 66, p. 60.)

* Median wage or salary not available for occupation group with fewer than 75,000 workers.

When a woman goes out to work, not only is she offered approximately half the salary of a man with equivalent training and ability, but she also finds herself the last hired and the first fired. In 1966 the male rate of unemployment was 3.3 while the female rate was 4.9. Furthermore, when a woman does get a job, her chances for a promotion and for moving over to a position of greater responsibility or importance, regardless of her qualifications, are much lower than those of her male co-workers. On the whole, women workers are at the same employment disadvantage as are members of minority groups. In fact, the March 1970 *Manpower Report of the*

President says that in the year 1969 the Equal Employment Opportunity Commission received reports of sex discrimination at a rate second only to those of race discrimination.

In the face of these frequently overwhelming obstacles to complete self-fulfillment through employment, there is little wonder why so many women have turned to motherhood. The fact of the matter is that these women do find a greater sense of personal worth in their activities as mothers than in the menial and financially thankless jobs that the *de facto* employment discrimination against women forces them into. The most unfortunate result of this discrimination is that all too often women become justifiably disillusioned and disappointed with their jobs and accept motherhood merely as the lesser of two evils.

Fortunately, the women's liberation movement, regardless of what opinion one holds toward it, has undeniably created an atmosphere in which women can fight for and demand their employment rights. In addition the feminist movement has also heightened the awareness of women to the degree where they realize that they no longer have to humbly accept second-rate jobs.

The Myth of the Working Mother

Increasingly, women who honestly wish to have children and yet cannot see themselves spending ten or more years cloistered in the home are deciding to combine motherhood with a career.

Maternal employment can definitely be considered an alternative to motherhood, since it questions the widely held belief that in order to be a good parent a woman must spend all her waking hours with her children. Unfortunately, although more and more mothers are taking this alternative to straight domestic life, there is still a strong residual feeling in our culture that when a woman has children, her place is in the home. And it is this feeling that maintains the Myth of the Working Mother.

Essentially, the myth rests on four assumptions: 1. the woman who works is likely to have maladjusted and delinquent children; 2. working mothers are responsible for the disintegration of family life; 3. the strain of maintaining a dual role as mother and worker jeopardizes a woman's mental health; and 4. women who work are forced to do so because their husbands are unable to provide adequately for their families. While these statements may seem to embody good common sense, psychologists, psychiatrists, and sociologists who have studied the question of maternal employment insist that they are pure myth.

Dr. Lee G. Burchinal and Dr. Jack E. Rossman, in their extensive study, "Relations Among Maternal Employment Indices and Developmental Characteristics of Children," found that among the 709 seventh-grade boys and girls and the 520 eleventh-grade boys and girls whose mothers had worked for specified periods of time, ". . . that maternal employment . . . had no apparent relationship with the personality, school-related or social developmental characteristics of the children. . . ."*

* L. G. Burchinal and J. E. Rossman, "Relations Among Maternal Employment Indices and Developmental Characteristics of Children," *Marriage and Family Living* (November, 1961), p. 339.

183

The Case Against Having Children

Burchinal and Rossman also state:

> If maternal employment during pre-school years of children's lives had negative effects upon the children's development, these effects were not observed by techniques used in this study.*

These opinions are supported by Dr. Kathryn Summers Powell in her study, "Maternal Employment in Relation to Family Life."

> Evidence offered by this investigation fails to support criticism of the relationship of maternal employment to children's personality development. The present study lends further support to the conclusion that there is a lack of evidence which would support the conception of the neglected, maladjusted child of middle-class employed mothers.**

It is interesting to note that Dr. Powell *does* find that children of employed mothers tend to have higher achievement motives than children of full-time housewives. We could speculate that by observing the desire of their working mothers to achieve more out of life than the traditional wife-mother role permits, these children learn that they too can strive for and achieve things over and above what may be considered average.

For those mothers who hesitate to combine a career with childbearing because they fear that, left unsupervised, their children will become delinquents, we have

* Loc. cit.
** Kathryn Summers Powell, "Maternal Employment in Relation to Family Life," *Marriage and Family Living* (November, 1961), p. 352.

these comforting words. Every available study done in the past ten years indicates that there is no statistically significant relationship between maternal employment and juvenile delinquency. Many psychologists agree that it is not the quantity of time a mother spends hawkishly watching her children that keeps them out of trouble, but the quality of the interaction between parent and child, the values that parents instill in their offspring, and the trust that parents show toward their children.

The Myth of the Working Mother tells us that tradition has given women the responsibility of keeping the family a closely knit unit. Once the woman leaves the home for the office, the myth goes on to say, the family begins to fall apart. Many women would like to believe this because it makes their functioning in the domestic area seem more important and thus adds a kind of status to the role of housewife and full-time mother. But if we look a little closer, we find that the old segmented family structure of the working father and the homebound mother is not nearly as good as many people believe it to be, and that in fact by working outside the home, a mother may actually be improving the quality of the relationships among the members of her family. Writing in the *Journal of Marriage and the Family*, Dr. Robert O. Blood, Jr., says:

> . . . the shape of the American Family is being altered by the exodus of women into the labor market. The role of men and women are converging for both adults and children. As a result, the family will be far less segmented internally, far less stratified into different age generations and different sexes. This will enable

family members to share more of the activities of life together, both work activities and play activities.

The old symmetry of male-dominated, female-serviced family life is being replaced by a new symmetry, both between husbands and wives and between brothers and sisters. To this emerging symmetry, the dual employment of mothers as well as fathers is a major contributor.*

For many women the responsibilities of keeping a home and raising children *seem* to be more than enough to keep them busy while the thought of working and homemaking appears to be an exercise in physical and psychological masochism. But as one psychiatrist with an admittedly lucrative suburban housewife trade said:

Many of the housewives I come in contact with often look for things to do to keep themselves busy. . . . they lint-pick and keep their homes super-clean. They buy endless cookbooks and prepare meals that take hours of preparation . . . and they become overinvolved in their children's activities to the point of obstructing their emotional development. . . . one reason for all this is that they're bored and they have to do something to combat the feeling of uselessness.

I know of any number of women who take naps during the day as a way of avoiding their frustrations . . . then there are those who read endlessly or involve themselves in charities in which they have no particular interest other than giving them something to

* Robert O. Blood, Jr., "Long-Range Causes and Consequences of the Employment of Married Women," *Journal of Marriage and the Family* (February, 1963). p. 47.

do. Sure many housewives claim they're tired at the end of the day. They're tired of marking time; they're tired of being bored to death.

Indeed the strain of boredom has caused many women to reevaluate their lives and to seek stimulation outside the home. But for others, cultural pressure keeps them from taking this alternative creating psychological stresses of a special nature. Psychiatrist Horace Gray, in his article "Trapped Housewife," discusses a possible cause for the problems that might bring women to the psychiatrist's couch:

> None of the respondents included had a job other than that of homemaker, therefore the resulting stress was not conflict between home and career, which so commonly is presumed in women's magazines as the principal result of opposites. The strain is fulfillment of the role of devoted mother demanded by other women in our modern society versus the need for self-development. The latter human right too commonly regarded askance as selfishness, and therefore attended by a feeling of guilt over imagined or actual neglect of children, or possible lack of normal self-assertion. It is one of the commonest anxieties to lead women into psychotherapy. . . .*

Rather than increasing tensions for women, maternal employment probably goes a long way toward providing them with additional outlets for their emotions through creative and meaningful self-expression. No doubt that a working mother will feel tired at the end of the day, but

* Horace Gray, "Trapped Housewife," *Journal of Marriage and the Family* (May, 1962), p. 181.

The Case Against Having Children

it will not be the futile tiredness of boredom, but instead the need for a well-earned rest.

In closing, we would like to put to rest the idea that most women who work are forced to do so because their husbands are incapable of supporting them and their children. This false belief has acted as a barrier to maternal employment because many husbands refuse to let their wives work for fear of being thought of as unable to meet their obligations to their families. And many women who fear that their husbands would feel emasculated if they worked, stay home so as not to deflate their husbands' egos. In truth, financial need does not play as large a part in maternal employment as is generally believed. A study done in 1961 by Mildred W. Weil isolated the factors influencing women's decisions to work. The following table summarizes the results of this study:

	Part-Time N = 26*	Full-Time N = 23	Total N = 49
Outside stimulation	23.2%	21.8%	11
Additional income	30.7	30.4	15
Job offered	11.5	0.0	3
Additional income and outside stimulation	7.7	21.8	7
Enjoy occupation	11.5	4.3	4
Husband disabled	0.0	4.3	1
Utilize education and training	15.4	17.4	8

(Source: Mildred W. Weil, "An Analysis of Factors Influencing Married Women's Actual or Planned Work Participation," *American Sociological Review*, vol. 26, no. 1, page 96. Used by permission.

* The letter "N" is used to indicate the number of subjects in the study.

While additional income did account for approximately 30 percent of the factors influencing women to work, it was far outweighed by the factors of outside stimulation, the desire to utilize education and training, and enjoyment of occupation. It becomes obvious then that women work for the same reasons as men, and to deny them the opportunity in order to preserve a false standard of masculinity and femininity is both irrational and unfair.

All we have done here is to take potshots at the Myth of the Working Mother, but we would like to recommend two excellent books that cover this area in depth. The first is *So You Want to Be a Working Mother* by Lois Benjamin, and the second is *The Case for the Working Mother* by Dorothy Whyte Cotton. Both of these volumes answer the many questions that women ask when considering the possibility of seeking an alternative to traditional motherhood.

We have emphasized the fact that the obstacles to maternal alternatives are largely social and cultural in nature and not biologically inherent in females. This, however, does not make them simple to overcome. The old ideas, the erroneous beliefs about the "proper place for women," and the entire psychological outlook of men and women must be overhauled before women can objectively and freely decide if they would rather have a career than children, or if they would like to combine working and childbearing. This is a major task, but it has to start somewhere if women are to be truly liberated members of society. A good starting point is suggested by Professor John J. Pietrofesa:

The Case Against Having Children

Teachers and counselors must accept and think of a woman as a responsible human being free to develop in whatever direction her abilities take her. Each individual must achieve a sense of personal worth and value or she will be unable to function fully as a human being. Self-fulfillment for women is not an absurd and irrational dream; it can and must be achieved.*

* *Women and the World of Work*, p. 259.

Appendix

The Maternal
Attitude Form

Have you ever thought about why you are a mother, or why you would like to be one some day? Chances are that you haven't. For most women, motherhood is, or appears to be, a natural occurrence in the course of their lives; an almost inescapable event biologically determined by the very fact that they are women. However, there are countless psychological, social, and cultural influences which, from earliest childhood, have acted upon women and structured their attitudes toward themselves and the roles they will play in society. Among these, the *maternal attitude*—the complex pattern of beliefs, needs, wants, and desires that motivates women to have children—is doubtless the most important.

Simply defined, an attitude is a tendency or disposition on the part of a person to believe, evaluate, or judge a concept, person, or thing based on that person's prior life experiences. Thus, when a woman becomes a mother she is motivated to do so by the set of beliefs, psychological needs and desires, and socio-cultural expectations that form her attitude toward children and the institution of motherhood.

In the course of researching *The Case Against Having Children* women offered us a great range of opinions about motherhood. And for many of them, their opinions helped motivate them to have children. To our way of thinking, some of these maternal attitudes seemed more desirable than others but being victims of our own biases we thought it would be interesting and valuable to get the opinions of various recognized experts in the behavioral sciences as to the desirability or undesirability of such attitudes toward motherhood. With the invaluable advice and assistance of psychologist Dr. Thomas Gilbart, Assistant Director of Counseling at Manhattan College, a preliminary list of 51 statements expressing prevalent attitudes toward motherhood, childbearing, and childrearing was constructed and submitted to the following panel of five distinguished behavioral scientists:

Dan Dodson, Ph.D., Sociologist. Dr. Dodson is a Professor of Education at the New York University School of Education.

Robert Gould., M.D., Psychiatrist. Dr. Gould is Director of Adolescent Services, Bellevue Psychiatric Hospital; Associate Professor Psychiatry, New York University Medical Center; and author of "The Wrong Reasons to Have Children" which appeared in the *New York Times Magazine*.

Rebecca Liswood, M.D., Marriage Counselor. Dr. Liswood is an Adjunct Professor at Adelphi University, teaching marriage and child care, and human sexuality; author of *A Marriage Doctor Speaks Her Mind About Sex*; and a practicing marriage counselor.

Margaret Mead, Ph.D., Anthropologist. Dr. Mead is a Curator Emeritus of Ethnology at the American Museum of Natural History, and a world-renowned lecturer and author. Dr. Mead's most recent book is *Culture and Commitment: A Study of the Generation Gap*.

Anthony J. Summo, Ph.D., Psychologist. Dr. Summo is Chairman of the Department of Psychology at Manhattan College and a practicing psychologist.

Each panel member was individually asked to rate the desirability or undesirability of each attitude statement. By desirability we mean that a particular statement expresses, in the opinion of the judge, a realistic evaluation of the role of mother; an understanding of the relationship between parent and child; and an awareness of the social, psychological and cultural roles that women can play. By undesirable, we mean that a particular attitude is faulty in terms of what a woman can expect from motherhood; exhibits an incomplete understanding of what is or is not biologically, socially, or emotionally inherent in the desire to be a mother; and is generally a poor reason to have children. Neither "desirable" nor "undesirable" ratings indicate value judgments in terms of a woman's ability to raise her children or to be a good mother. The panel used a scale of one (1) to eleven (11) to rate each attitude statement. A rating of one (1) meant that a particular item was totally *desirable*, while number two (2) through five (5) denoted lesser degrees of desirability. At the other end of the scale, a rating of eleven (11) meant that an item was *totally undesirable*, while numbers ten (10) down to seven (7) indicated lesser degrees of undesirability. An item was rated with a six (6) if a panel member had neutral feelings toward it. No single item had the unanimous agreement of the panel, but of the 51 original statements 30 did evoke a strong consensus. A mean score for each of these 30 items was arrived at by averaging the panel's individual responses. The result was a mean or average rating for each statement which indicated the panel's overall opinion as to an item's desirability or undesirability.

To see how your attitudes toward motherhood compare with those of the panel, read each of the following statements. If you find that a particular statement expresses an attitude that you believe a woman *should* have toward motherhood, check "desirable." But, if a statement expresses what you feel is unacceptable, check "undesirable." If an item does not exactly correspond to your feelings, check the response that most closely approximates your attitude. Remember, there are no right or wrong answers and you are just comparing your opinions with those of the panel.

1. Nowadays, parents have the social responsibility not to have large families.　　　　( ) Desirable
　　　　　　　　　　　　　　　　( ) Undesirable
2. People would probably think I had some physical

problem if I remained childless.

( ) Desirable
( ) Undesirable

3. If I did not have children I
would be lonely in my old
age.

( ) Desirable
( ) Undesirable

4. A young couple should wait
about four years before they
decide to have children.

( ) Desirable
( ) Undesirable

5. Women who do not have
children are going against
nature.

( ) Desirable
( ) Undesirable

6. The desire of a couple's
parents for grandchildren
should not play a part in
their decision to have children.

( ) Desirable
( ) Undesirable

7. If I did not have a child I
would feel as though I were
a social outcast.

( ) Desirable
( ) Undesirable

8. Sexual relations are sinful if
children are not desired.

( ) Desirable
( ) Undesirable

9. If I did not have children I
would be selfish.

( ) Desirable
( ) Undesirable

10. Adoption is a poor alternative to having your own
children.

( ) Desirable
( ) Undesirable

11. I would not feel truly feminine if I never had children.

( ) Desirable
( ) Undesirable

12. I would be just as happy if
my daughter chooses a ca-
reer instead of motherhood.

( ) Desirable
( ) Undesirable

The Case Against Having Children

13. Love alone is not sufficient to be a good parent.

( ) Desirable
( ) Undesirable

14. A woman's capability to bear children does not also mean that she has the capability to raise them.

( ) Desirable
( ) Undesirable

15. I believe that a woman should have the right to terminate an unwanted pregnancy.

( ) Desirable
( ) Undesirable

16. Children should be encouraged to be independent, even if it means that they will go against their parents' wishes.

( ) Desirable
( ) Undesirable

17. Expectant mothers should read several books on child raising in order to learn the experts' opinions.

( ) Desirable
( ) Undesirable

18. Without children my life would be wasted.

( ) Desirable
( ) Undesirable

19. Women should become mothers because that is their traditional role in society.

( ) Desirable
( ) Undesirable

20. I do not believe that large-family mothers can give their children the same quality of attention as a small-family mother.

( ) Desirable
( ) Undesirable

21. Becoming a mother is the best way for a young married woman to develop into a mature and responsible adult.

( ) Desirable
( ) Undesirable

22. Husbands and wives can have a great deal in common even if they do not have children.

( ) Desirable
( ) Undesirable

23. If a doctor's examination found that the fetus I was carrying was severely malformed I would probably seek an abortion.

( ) Desirable
( ) Undesirable

24. Childbearing is not a God-given obligation that all women must assume.

( ) Desirable
( ) Undesirable

25. There are many valuable contributions that women can make to the world instead of children.

( ) Desirable
( ) Undesirable

26. Personally, I do not think there is anything wrong with a woman who does not desire children.

( ) Desirable
( ) Undesirable

27. It is a good idea for women to combine motherhood with such outside pursuits as a part-time job or continued education.

( ) Desirable
( ) Undesirable

28. I believe that my hopes and aspirations can be expressed through my children.

( ) Desirable
( ) Undesirable

29. Having a baby is generally not a good way to cure a troubled marriage.

( ) Desirable
( ) Undesirable

30. I can understand how certain women would derive more self-satisfaction from a career than from motherhood.

( ) Desirable
( ) Undesirable

Listed below are the panel's responses to each item. In parentheses are the *average ratings* given each attitude statement. These indicate the degree of desirability or undesirability relative to the eleven-point scale that the judges used in evaluating the items.

1. Desirable (*Panel average: 1.4*)
2. Undesirable (*Panel average: 7.8*)
3. Undesirable (*Panel average: 7.6*)
4. Desirable (*Panel average: 2.2*)
5. Undesirable (*Panel average: 8.2*)
6. Desirable (*Panel average: 1.8*)
7. Undesirable (*Panel average: 9.0*)
8. Undesirable (*Panel average: 9.0*)
9. Undesirable (*Panel average: 8.6*)
10. Undesirable (*Panel average: 7.4*)
11. Undesirable (*Panel average: 8.0*)
12. Desirable (*Panel average: 2.6*)
13. Desirable (*Panel average: 2.4*)

14. Desirable *(Panel average: 2.6)*
15. Desirable *(Panel average: 2.0)*
16. Desirable *(Panel average: 3.0)*
17. Desirable *(Panel average: 2.0)*
18. Undesirable *(Panel average: 7.0)*
19. Undesirable *(Panel average: 7.6)*
20. Desirable *(Panel average: 2.4)*
21. Undesirable *(Panel average: 7.2)*
22. Desirable *(Panel average: 3.0)*
23. Desirable *(Panel average: 3.0)*
24. Desirable *(Panel average: 2.8)*
25. Desirable *(Panel average: 3.2)*
26. Desirable *(Panel average: 3.0)*
27. Desirable *(Panel average: 2.8)*
28. Undesirable *(Panel average: 7.2)*
29. Desirable *(Panel average: 3.0)*
30. Desirable *(Panel average: 2.2)*

The 30 item Maternal Attitude Form was given to a sample group of 28 mothers and 19 non-mothers. Their general responses to the statements may be summarized as follows:

✻ The 24 college-educated women in the sample group showed an overwhelming tendency to agree with the experts' opinions, while the 23 women who had never attended college showed only a slight tendency to agree with the experts' opinions.

✻ The 19 women who indicated that they agreed with the women's liberation contention that there is no biological or psychological justification for the distinctions that our society makes between the male role and the female role were in *97 percent accord* with the panel's opinions, while the 28 women who disagreed with the feminist point of view had an average agreement rate with the panel of 68 percent.

✳ Large-family mothers, those with more than 3 children, showed only a slight tendency to agree with the experts while those with small-families showed a significantly higher rate of agreement.

✳ Working mothers in the sample group showed a much stronger tendency to agree with the panel than did the non-working mothers.

✳ Among the childless women who indicated that they definitely planned to have children, the average rate of agreement with the panel was 78 percent. Those childless women who indicated that they were uncertain about their childbearing plans agreed with the experts at a rate of 92 percent. And those who stated that they definitely did not want to have children were in 100 percent accord with the panel's opinions.

There are several conclusions that may be drawn from these findings. The first is that higher education affects a woman's attitudes toward motherhood. The more educated a woman is the less likely she is to view motherhood as the "proper" role for all women and the more likely she is to see that there are alternatives to motherhood. On the other hand, women with less education—and this doesn't mean less intelligence—are more apt to accept the conventional wife-mother role and to choose mother-hood rather than careers or professions as their means for self-fulfillment and self-actualization. On the whole, it would be safe to say that women who have *not* gone to college are more traditional in their attitudes concerning motherhood and the role of women in society than are college-educated women who take a somewhat broader view of the functioning of women in our culture. This was supported by the fact that of the 19 women who expressed sympathy for the feminist ideology, 18 were college graduates.

Second, large-family mothers appear to be more con-ventional in their attitudes toward motherhood than are small-family mothers. Their beliefs—as indicated by their responses to certain items on the Maternal Attitude Form —that childbearing is an important part of femininity, that children are vehicles through which they can express their hopes and aspirations, and that without children their lives would be wasted, are the strong motivational factors that led them to have large families. Furthermore, their overall responses to the Maternal Attitude Form clearly showed that they are convinced that a woman's place *is* in the home. In contrast to this, small-family mothers tended to believe that women could be mothers or career women, and that satisfaction and fulfillment does not necessarily come from staying at home and raising children. This was borne out by the fact that while all but one of the eight large-family mothers did not work, eight of the 20 small-family mothers worked either part-time or full-time in jobs outside the home.

The third and final conclusion is that age may play a part in a woman's attitude toward motherhood. All of the childless women, whose average age was 23, tended to show a high degree of agreement with the experts—including those who eventually planned to have children. This might be a result of the increasing awareness among young women today that the institutions of society—business, higher education, and the professions—open to them are expanding and that motherhood is no longer the only role that offers them status, prestige, recognition, and a feeling of accomplishment and usefulness.

Now, how do these findings relate to you? It would be safe to assume that if you tended to *disagree* with the panel, or if you had only a slight tendency to agree with the experts' opinions, that you are probably a somewhat conventional woman who believes that females should occupy the traditional social role of wife and mother. For you, children are a very necessary and important part of your life and you are likely to believe that most women would find their highest degree of self-fulfillment within the institution of motherhood. An educated guess would be that you are hard-pressed to understand why a married woman would not want to have children. On the other hand, if your responses tended to coincide rather frequently with those of the panel, chances are that you can accept the emerging modern view that female self-fulfillment and self-actualization do not reside only in the home and in the nursery. You might also be the type of woman who is actively questioning the validity of the belief that all women are emotionally equipped for motherhood by mere virtue of the fact that they have the

physical capability to reproduce. And although you your-
self may have children or expect to have children, you
see nothing wrong with a woman who remains childless
in order to pursue alternatives to motherhood.

Index

Index

Index

208

Index

Maternal overprotection, meaning of, 28-29
Maturity, four kinds of, 51-54
Mead, Dr. Margaret, 193
Men Our Masters, organization of, 18
Meyrowitz, Joseph H., 146, 146n
Miller, Dr. O. J., 13
M.O.M., 18
Monahan, Thomas, 138-139, 139n
Monopoly as reason for fatherhood, 90-92
Montagu, Ashley, 153-154, 154n, 162, 162n, 174-175
Moore, Bernice Milburn, 120-121, 121n
Motherhood, alternatives to, 149-189 (see also "Alternatives to motherhood")
"Motherhood; Who Needs It?" 9, 10, 10n
Motherhood, wrong reasons for, 38-82
　to achieve "adulthood," 51-54
　for activity, 59-61
　to compensate for unhappy childhood, 48-51
　feeling of pregnancy, enjoyment of, 68-72
　guilt and pain dependence motive, 66-68
　for insurance in old age, 56-59
　"outsider," to avoid consideration as, 75-79
　for particular attention, 63-66
　as personal fulfillment, 39-40
　to please parents, 72-75
　for proof of sexual maturity, 54-57
　for punishment, 66-68
　for recognition, 40-43
　from religion, 79-82
　to save marriage, 43-48

Namath, Joe, "female," possibility of having, 155-156
Natalism, dangers of, 96-129 (see also "Families, large, case against")
National Institute of Mental Health, 128
Natural Superiority of Women, The, 153-154, 154n, 162, 162n, 175, 175n

Neiger, Ira, 55, 91
New Republic, 31n, 104n
"New Roles for Men and Women," 179-180, 180n
New York Times Magazine, 91-92, 92n, 117-118, 118n, 122n, 128n, 192
New York University, 1
1984, 111

Object of sexual instinct, 12
O'Connor, L. R., 11-12
Occupational inferiority complex of women, 165-172
　secondary work motives, 167-170
Old age insurance, having child as, 56-59
"On the Need to Be Pregnant," 63-64, 64n
Option Limitation, meaning of, 18-23
Oregon State University, 98
Orthodox Jew, pressure upon from religion to bear children, 79-82
Orwell, George, 111
"Outsider," having child to avoid consideration as, 75-79
"Over Populated America," 30-31, 31n, 104n
Overprotection, maternal, meaning of, 28-29
Ovesey, Dr. Lionel, 165-166, 166n
Ozymandias, 94

Paleolithic era, beginning of differentiation of roles in, 3
"Parenthood as Crises," 141n
Parents, pleasing as reason for bearing children, 72-75
"Penis envy" as reason for desiring pregnancy, 68-70
Perpetuation of family name as reason for fatherhood, 93-95
Personal freedoms, limitation of in societies with large populations, 113-116
Personal problems, having child to solve, 39-40
Phi Beta Kappan, 116n
Photographic Manual of Sexual Intercourse, 11
Physical problems for mothers of large families, 129
Pid-yon-a-ben, meaning of, 79

Index